Poultry on the Grill

Poultry

on the Grill

by *Phyllis Magida* and *Barbara Grunes*

A DELL TRADE PAPERBACK

DEDICATION

This book is dedicated to Barry Bluestein and Kevin Morrissey,
our friends at Season to Taste Books, Ltd.

ACKNOWLEDGMENTS

We would like to acknowledge the assistance of
Michelle Chroman and Mary Westergrad.

Contents

Birds of a Feather

Birds of a Different Feather

Recipe Listing by Type of Poultry

Chicken

Whole
Chinese Tea-Smoked Chicken
Grilled Free-Range Chicken with Mace Sauce and Bread
    Stuffing
Perfect Grilled Chicken with Five Sauces

Parts
Barbecued Chicken in a Garlic Bread Basket
Basket of Breaded Chicken and Turkey Nuggets with
    Barbecue Sauce
Buffalo Chicken Wings
Chicken Kabobs with Orange Butter
Chicken Legs Stuffed with Apples, Raisins and Rum
Chicken Quarters with Tart Lemon Sauce
Chicken Teriyaki
Drumsticks with Bay Leaves
Five-Spice Chicken Wings
Grilled Drumsticks with Five-Minute Barbecue Sauce
Italian Sausage–Stuffed Drumsticks with Smoky Pizza
    Bread
Korean Lettuce Sandwiches
Korean Red Chicken
Smoked Honeyed Chicken with Kumquat Slivers
Smoked Honey-Mustard Chicken with Noodle Pudding
Transylvanian Grilled Chicken

Breasts
Blackened Chicken Breasts with Sour Cream and Chives
Chicken Breasts with Mustard–Crème Fraîche Sauce
Chicken Breasts Stuffed with Cornbread and Hot Sausage
Chicken Kabobs with Orange Butter
Chicken and Livers Yakitori
Grilled Chicken Breasts with Moroccan Stuffing
Grilled Stuffed Chicken Turnovers
Murghi Malai Kabab (Indian Chicken Kabobs)

Already cooked (leftover)
Chicken Tostadas with Hot Green Salsa
Chicken or Turkey Chili
Chicken with Whole-Wheat Pasta and Pine Nuts
Grilled Chicken Muffuletta
Grilled Chicken Risotto
Smoked Turkey, Pecan and Fresh Raspberry Salad
Warm Smoked Duck Salad with Garlic Croutons

Livers
Chicken Liver Kabobs with Garlic and Mint
Chicken and Livers Yakitori

Capon

Tom Jones's Capon

Cornish Hen

Butterflied Cornish Hens with Grilled Papaya
Grilled Cornish Hens with Fragrant Fruit Sauce

Turkey

Barbecued Turkey Drumsticks (Caveman Party)
Basket of Breaded Chicken and Turkey Nuggets with
    Barbecue Sauce
Easy-Grilled Turkey Thighs with Picante Sauce
Smoked Turkey Breast with Pecan Butter
Smoked Turkey with Winter Fruit Relish
Thanksgiving Grilled Turkey with Apricot Bread Stuffing
Turkey Chunks with Two Sauces
Turkey with Cinnamon-Raisin Bread Stuffing
Turkey and Fig Kabobs with Hot Fig Sauce
Turkey Ovals on Heated Rolls
Turkey Sausages on Sticks
Turkey Strips with Spicy Peanut Sauce

Duck

Duck Pieces with Beer Barbecue Baste and Grilled Peppers
Duck Quarters with Kumquat–Brandy Basting Sauce

Duck Quarters with Quince Brushing Sauce and Baby Vegetables
Duck Quarters with Two-Peppercorn Sauce
Duck with Hungarian Red Pepper Sauce
Ducks on a Spit with Lime Marmalade Baste and Chilled
   Mango Puree
Grilled Whole Duck with Fennel
Sliced Duck Breast on Rye Bread
Smoked Long Island Duck with Apple and Crème Fraîche Sauce
Smoked Long Island Duck with Mandarin Orange Sauce
Smoked Long Island Duck, Peking Style

Goose

Goose on a Spit
Grilled Christmas Goose

Game

Mallard
Grilled Mallards on a Bed of Warm Sauerkraut
Grilled Mallard with Green Salsa
Smoked Mallard with Homemade Plum Sauce

Partridge
Partridge in Crème Fraîche with Oranges and
   Pomegranates
Spit-Grilled Partridge with Prune Sauce

Pheasant
Grilled Pheasant with Peach Cumberland Sauce
Pheasant with Grilled Chestnuts and Chestnut Sauce

Poussin
Butterflied Poussin with Sun-Dried Tomatoes
Grilled Poussin in Applejack and Cream
Poussin, Middle Eastern Style, with Currant Stuffing

Quail
Quail Adovada with Blue Cornbread Madeleines
Quail with Grilled Pineapple Slices and Pineapple Sauce
Spit-Grilled Quail with Pistachio Butter

Squab
Grilled Squab with Pepita Spread and Stuffed Baby
   Pumpkins

Introduction

"Poultry is for the cook what a canvas is for the painter."
—JEAN ANTHELME BRILLAT–SAVARIN

Brillat-Savarin was right. But if today's cooks spent all the time that 19th-century cooks did making and cleaning up from their culinary works of art, we would go hungry.

This doesn't mean we want our food to be less good than it was in the past, or less beautiful, or less well made. What we want is food that is easy to prepare and clean up after.

All of this brings us to the ultraspecial collection of recipes in this book. Poultry is our canvas, and it includes tame game as well as domestic chicken, turkey, duck and goose. Our method of cooking—grilling—makes for easy cleaning, quick preparation and elegant presentation. (We've included indoor stove adaptations as well in the event you don't like snow-barbecuing.)

In case you're wondering where these wonderful things—the poultry, game and grill—come from, the chicken was domesticated around 2500 B.C. and is descended from the red jungle fowl of Southeast Asia, the turkey is indigenous to North America and the duck came here from China.

Many game birds were brought here as oddities from Asia and Europe, but stayed and thrived. Today game is raised on farms all over the United States.

No one knows who first invented the grill, but the word *barbecue* is credited to two different groups: the Caribbean Arawak Indians, who grill over grids made of green twigs called *barbacoa*, and French chefs, whose term *barbe à queue* means "beard to tail" and describes the way in which a whole bird or animal is spitted.

All of the fowl called for in this book is readily available: Chicken (broiler/fryers, capons and Cornish hens) as well as turkey and domestic duck are sold in supermarkets. The mallard, guinea hen, pheasant, squab, wild turkey, free-range chicken, poussin, quail and partridge that had to be hunted for a few years back are now available in specialty shops, by mail and even in some city markets, already trussed and cleaned. The supermarket poultry is even available in parts, ranging from turkey legs and steaks to boneless breasts to chicken wings.

Grilling is a very versatile cooking technique, and we've designed this book to help you make the most of it. You will find sections herein on smoked poultry, the under-30-minute grill, appetizers, feasts, kabobs and whole birds.

We've ranged and rummaged through the regions of the world's cuisines so we could include specialties—all grill adapted—such as Transylvanian chicken with garlic to fend off vampires, Smoked Peking Long Island Duck and Quail Adovada with Blue Cornbread Madeleines, which we adapted from Santa Fe.

You will be especially pleased to find certain types of poultry not previously thought to be grill-friendly. Mallard, for example, has the reputation of having a tougher-than-chicken texture. And Long Island duck has a high fat content. But we found that farm-raised birds—from no fat to low fat—can be grilled perfectly over direct heat because they are more tender (less muscular) than their wild counterparts.

We've even found a way to coax the fat out of goose and duck before grilling or smoking, by poaching the bird in simmering water for 3 minutes, then hanging it with string from the showerhead over a dripping pan placed in the tub.

You will find other unusual practices here, too. We put stuffings between the skin and the meat of poultry—a cornbread/sausage mixture is stuffed under the skin of individual chicken breast halves, and a delicious pecan butter is smoothed under the breast skin of a boned turkey roast, among many others. This method keeps the flesh unbelievably moist and succulent during grilling, and it flavors the meat in a special way.

We roast whole garlic cloves on the grill, too, then suggest you squeeze their soft, delicious interiors directly onto hot slices of grilled chicken. We soak our aromatics—whole cloves and oregano leaves, for example—in water so they last longer when thrown on the hot coals.

Take a look through "The Basics" before you try out a recipe. You will find charts detailing the taste and texture of tame game and domestic birds and focusing on grilling times and methods. You will find a discussion of poultry in general and an overview of grills, fuels and methods of grill-cooking. And don't overlook the list of mail-order sources for unusual ingredients or the list of recipes by bird type.

Here's to glorious grilled poultry of all kinds. We feel sure you will enjoy each preparation and savor each dish as much as we did when creating and testing them for you.

The Basics

Grilling poultry is both simple and tricky. Read this chapter before you start and refer to it as you develop your skills. With a thorough knowledge of the basics, you'll find experimenting and innovating a breeze.

Poultry, Grills and Other Essentials

About Poultry

Poultry of all kinds is increasing in popularity in this country; chicken sales will surpass beef sales for the first time ever in 1989; farm-raised game is also increasing in popularity. There are several reasons for this. First of all, most poultry is just delicious, whether grilled and served plain or ladled with a sumptuous sauce. Poultry is also low in calories and cholesterol—even those birds with fat under the skin, as long as the fat and skin are not eaten.

Dark meat has slightly more calories than light meat, no matter what bird is being eaten. Poultry remains much lower in calories than beef, however. A three-ounce serving of filet mignon has about 300 calories. Compare this to three ounces of roasted, skinless white meat chicken, which contains only 116 calories, or to the 131 calories in the same amount of dark meat. Three ounces of skinless white meat turkey has only 119 calories—with the dark meat coming in only slightly higher at 142 calories per three ounces.

Light and dark meat is caused by differing amounts of myoglobin, an oxygen-storing substance found in meat, which is present in the muscles. Dark meat muscles, which are used a good deal, need a lot of oxygen, so they contain myoglobin in large quantities.

Here are a few tips to remember when cooking today's tame game and domestic poultry.

- When barbecuing any presauced poultry directly over hot coals, be sure to turn it every few minutes. So much barbecued poultry is served with a blackened, charred exterior and a raw interior because the heat burns the sugar in the barbecue sauce. If you turn your poultry often, it will never char.

- Test a chicken for doneness by inserting a fork into the thick part of the meat, usually the thigh. If the juices run clear, the chicken is done. If the juices are pink, the chicken is not yet done. You may sometimes find, as you cut into the meat, that the meat near the bone looks bloody; this does not mean that the chicken isn't cooked. The bloody-looking meat is caused by the red hemoglobin seeping out of the bone during grilling. This happens particularly in young chickens whose bones are still soft. It is perfectly safe to eat as is; if you continue grilling, you will overcook it.

- You can use an instant-read thermometer (a small thermometer attached to a shaft with a pointy probe tip) to test for doneness as well. Insert the probe tip into the thickest portion of the meat, such as the thigh in a whole bird, making sure that the tip is not touching the bone.

The chicken is done when the thermometer registers 180 degrees; but if you are cooking a whole chicken, take it off the grill when it is just a few degrees short of this temperature, as whole chickens, like large beef roasts, continue cooking for a few moments away from the heat.

The light meat of turkey is done when the thermometer registers 170 to 175 degrees, which is a full 10 degrees lower than was suggested a few years ago. Dark meat turkey, however,

Cut off the tips of *all* poultry wings—from quail to turkey—and store them in a closed plastic bag in the freezer for use in making chicken stock. TO USE: Put them in a saucepan with water to cover, add a few peppercorns, a quartered onion and a bay leaf. Heat to a boil and simmer for 45 to 60 minutes to make a rich stock.

should be cooked between 180 and 185 degrees. If you are grilling a whole turkey, you will have to cook it to 180 degrees, otherwise the legs won't be done. Take the whole turkey off the grill when the instant-read thermometer registers just a few degrees under 180.

- In the past, wild game was always served bloody—the French call it *sangnant*. With farm-raised game, the style is still to cook all dark meat birds so they are still pink inside near the bone. But the final decision about how long any bird should stay on the grill is up to you—the bird is only truly overcooked when the meat is dark and dry.

- Large pieces of poultry fresh from the grill (or oven) should sit at room temperature for 15 to 30 minutes before being carved. You will lose vital juices if you carve the meat too soon.

- You can avoid dirtying a bowl if you mix up the marinade in the same ziplock plastic bag in which you will eventually marinate the poultry pieces.

- You can ease grill cleanup by lining the grill with tin foil (shiny-side down) before placing the briquets in the grill. To clean after grilling, once the ashes are cool you can simply scoop them up along with the foil.

- Be sure to wash all poultry under cold running water before using it.

TIP: Never salt poultry before placing it on the grill—the salting draws out valuable juices.

Cooking Time Chart

Domestic

Type of Poultry	Portion	Portion Weight	Grilling Method	Time on Grill
Broiler/ Fryer	Whole	3 lb.	Indirect	1 hr.
	Whole	2½ lb.	Smoked	75 mins.
	Half	1¾ lb.	Smoked	70 mins.
	Quarter	10 oz.	Direct	25–30 mins.
	Breast half no wing	8 oz.	Direct	20–24 mins.
	Breast half boneless	4 oz.	Direct	9 mins.
	12 pieces	3–3½ lb. total (about 4 oz. each)	Direct	24 mins. (wings cook faster)
	Wings	4 oz.	Direct	15 mins.
	Drumsticks	⅓ lb.	Direct	24 mins.
	Kabobs	1½″ squares	Direct	10–12 mins.
	Kabob strips	3–4″ long	Direct	15–16 mins.
Capon	Whole	6 lb.	Indirect	3 hrs.
Cornish Hen	Whole	1½ lb.	Indirect	45 mins.
	Butterflied	1½ lb.	Direct	20 mins.
Duck	Whole	4–5 lb.	Poach/ smoked	1¾ hrs.
	Whole	4–5 lb.	Indirect	
	Whole	4–5 lb.	Rotisserie	2 hrs.
	12 pieces	4–5 lb.	Indirect	1½ hrs.
	Quarters	4–5 lb.	Indirect	1½ hrs.
Free-range Chicken	Whole	3½ lb.	Indirect	70 mins.
	12 pieces	3½ lb.	Direct	24 mins.

Domestic

Goose	Whole	9 lb.	Indirect	3 hrs.
	Whole	9 lb.	Rotisserie	3 hrs.
Poussin	Butterflied	1 lb.	Direct	16 mins.
Turkey	Whole	12–14 lb.	Indirect	2–2½ hrs.
	Whole	12 lb.	Smoked	5–7 hrs.
	Drumstick		Indirect	1 hr.
	Kabobs	1½" squares	Direct	10–12 mins.
	Kabob strips	3–4" long	Direct	15–16 mins.
	Boneless breast	3½ lb.	Smoked	2 hrs.
	Leg w/ Thigh	2–3 lb.		
Turkey (free-range)	Butterflied	12–14 lb.	Indirect	2–2½ hrs.

Tame Game

Type of Poultry	*Portion*	*Portion Weight*	*Grilling Method*	*Time on Grill*
Guinea Hen	Halves	1⅛–1¼ lb.	Direct	24 mins.
Mallard	Halves	1¼ lb. ea.	Direct	24 mins.
	Halves	1¼ lb. ea.	Smoked	1¾ hrs.
Partridge	Whole	1 lb.	Indirect	35–40 mins.
	Whole	1 lb.	Rotisserie	35–40 mins.
Pheasant	Halves	1⅛–1¼ lb.	Direct	24 mins.
Quail	Whole	4–6 oz.	Rotisserie	25–30 mins.
	Butterflied	4–6 oz.	Direct	10–15 mins.
Squab	Whole	1 lb.	Rotisserie	35–40 mins.
	Whole	1 lb.	Indirect	35–40 mins.

Grills

In its most basic form, barbecuing is simply food cooked in the heat and smoke of burning charcoal. The heat is transferred to the food by radiation: heat radiates in smoky waves from the hot charcoal and is absorbed by the food. When the grill is covered, the food is also cooked by convection: molecules of smoke and air create hot currents that circulate around the food, transferring the heat to it.

Keep a bottle filled with water near your grill to control flare-ups.

Barbecue grills range in size and cost from simple, shallow pans topped with grids, which cost as little as $6, to multifunction wagon-type grills boasting such luxuries as rotisseries and rangetop burners for making sauces, whose price tags can run into the hundreds.

If you are buying a new grill, be sure to take its size into consideration. If it's just you, your mate and the dog to feed, a small, inexpensive tabletop grill might be sufficient. But if you have a large family and neighbors who drop in or are used to lots of backyard entertaining, you will want to buy a grill with enough space to cook large quantities at the same time.

There are five basic types of grills.

Kettles and Covered Cookers

These grills are distinguished by their deep firepans and covers and two sets of dampers that control fire temprature. They come in three shapes: round (called kettles), which is most popular, square or rectangular (both of which are called covered cookers). Most have attached metal pans underneath the firepan dampers to catch ashes. Covered grills are extremely versatile. The cover cuts down on the amount of circulating oxygen, which prevents flare-ups and reduces the chances of burning. The cover also turns the grill into an oven that traps smoke and creates a smokier environment for food to cook in.

Most covered grills do not have height-adjustable grids, so everything must be grilled six inches away from the hot coals. Covered grills with height-adjustable grids do exist, but they are hard to find.

Covered grills range in size from small tabletop models to larger stand-up, backyard models. You can find a variety of features including built-in electric starters, fire doors, which let you add coals without removing the grid, rotisseries and shish kabob attachments.

These are the most versatile charcoal grills, allowing you to use either fast, direct grilling methods or slower, indirect methods (see "Cooking on the Grill," page 16). Hot smoking and water smoking can also be done on these grills (see "Water Smoking," page 18).

Oil the grid when cool; then place it over the charcoal and let it get hot before adding the food. This will give the food those attractive grid patterns that characterize grilled food.

Water Smokers

Water smokers have a cylindrical shape, which encourages the smoke to rise upward toward the food, and a water pan, which keeps food moist during smoking through water evaporation. Since poultry can take hours to smoke, charcoal must be replenished at regular intervals.

Braziers

These round grills have shallow firepans, often no more than 4 inches deep. Usually they have three parts: the legs, a firepan and a grid. They can be more elaborate with hoods and rotisserie attachments for cooking large chickens, ducks, pheasants or even geese and turkeys. Food cooked by rotisserie is especially succulent because the constant turning motion allows the food to baste itself with its own juices.

Gas and Electric Grills

These grills contain lava or other volcanic rocks, which are artificially heated by gas jets or electric heating elements. As the food cooks, the juices drip onto the volcanic rocks, vaporize from the heat and turn to smoke. It is this noncharcoal smoke that flavors food cooked on gas and electric grills.

Manufacturers of these grills insist that the flavor of food cooked over volcanic rock is as good as that cooked over burning charcoal. To test this, we bought a whole chicken breast, split it in half and brushed it with oil. We cooked one half on a charcoal grill and the other half on an electric grill. The one cooked on the electric grill in its own smoke was nicely flavored but did not have a charcoal flavor, while the one cooked over charcoal had an intense charcoal flavor.

These grills range in size from tabletop versions to large wagons big enough to feed a crowd, which can be pushed around on wheels in your backyard. Rotisserie attachments are available for all sizes, although the smaller ones are sometimes hard to find. Recent refinements include, among other things, a self-cleaning feature and an attached thermos drawer to chill drinks.

Portable or Tabletop Grills

These grills are distinguished by their short legs and small size. Available as covered kettles, braziers and gas and electric grills, they are terrific for picnics, beach parties and small gatherings. Some small gas and electric models even have rotisserie attachments. Fans rave about the portability and easy storage of small grills. If you live in a high-rise with a balcony or fire escape, this may be the grill for you, although some townships have strict fire regulations that may prohibit outdoor grilling in your building.

Fuels

There are several types of fuel available for grilling and various methods of lighting each type. We don't recommend crumpled newspaper or scrap wood kindling as there are many easier lighting methods which are just as effective.

Lump Charcoal

Lump charcoal is made by heating hardwoods, such as oak or cherry, to high temperatures in enclosed spaces with limited amounts of air. Under these conditions the wood glows but does not ignite. Moisture evaporates, driving out the acids, oils and tars. The resulting charcoal is irregular in size and shape and takes up more storage room than processed briquets. Devotees insist it burns hotter and stays hot longer than processed briquets, imparting only natural smoke smells to food. Lump charcoal is more expensive than the processed variety. The most popular lump charcoal is made with only mesquite hardwood and emits an unmistakable mesquite smoke when ignited.

Lump charcoal can be started successfully with electric starters, chimneys and compressed wood (see "Charcoal Starters," page 12). Using a chemical starter on this pure charcoal would be self-defeating.

^^^

Standard Charcoal Briquets

These are made of sawdust and leftover wood, heated in the same way as lump charcoal to burn off the acids, oils and tars. The charcoal is then ground to powder and combined with other materials such as starch and sawdust. The mixture is then formed into uniform briquets. Fans insist processed charcoal burns more evenly than lump charcoal, costs less and is more convenient to store.

Standard charcoal briquets can be started successfully with liquid chemical starters, electric starters, chimneys and compressed wood (see "Charcoal Starters," page 12).

Hickory Specialties, Inc., of Brentwood, Tennessee, manufactures charcoal briquets made from the by-products in making Jack Daniels whiskey. The briquets are made from the hardwood sugar-maple charcoal used in the whiskey's mellowing process. They do not impart a whiskey flavor but are said by the company to burn with a faintly sweet, woodsy odor.

Standard briquets mixed with mesquite chips are also available. They burn with a faint mesquite flavor.

Ignite as you would standard charcoal briquets.

Instant-Lighting Briquets

These are standard charcoal briquets that have been soaked in liquid chemicals to ensure that they ignite easily and quickly. Critics claim these briquets emit an unpleasant odor in the smoke and that it can be tasted in the food.

Ignite with matches.

Wood Chunks

There are several kinds of wood chunks on the market that can be used as an alternative to charcoal: hickory chunks, which give a strong, pungent, baconlike flavor (popular in the South, where they are used to smoke pork products); alder chunks, which impart a delicate woody flavor (popular in the Northwest, where they are used to smoke salmon); fruit wood chunks (apple, cherry and peach), which have a sweet, subtle woody flavor; and the ever-popular mesquite chunks (used in the Southwest), which give an unmistakably strong, rich flavor to food. Since mesquite wood chunks give a stronger mesquite flavor than all-mesquite charcoal, briquets with added mesquite chips or plain mesquite wood chips, we recommend that you don't use them with delicate poultry such as poussin.

Never throw cedar, fir, pine or spruce on the grill as the smoke they produce is unpleasantly bitter.

When the food has finished cooking, quickly cover the grill and close the vents to smother the fire—the remaining coals will go out and can be used again.

Ignite wood chunks of all kinds with electric starters, chimneys and compressed wood starters (see "Charcoal Starters," page 12). Using chemical starter on this pure wood fuel would be self-defeating. Soak all wood chunks in water for at least 30 minutes before use to create a smokier flavor.

Other Aromatics

A number of things produce fragrant smoke when thrown on burning charcoal. These include herbs such as basil and rosemary and spices such as cinnamon sticks, whole nutmegs and cloves. Citrus peels, which add a faint orangy flavor to food, can also be used. Soak all aromatics—fresh or dried—in water to saturate; they will create more smoke that way.

Wood Chips

Some types of wood chips work well as aromatics when added to charcoal. These include mesquite, hickory, peach, cherry, apple, alder and even kiawe wood from Hawaii. Soak the chips in water for 30 minutes before using so they will give off more smoke. This process is called cold smoking. (An even better way to cold smoke is to soak larger wood chunks—see "Fuels," page 9—in water and then to add them to the coals. Do not use more than six chunks at a time or they will put out the charcoal. Never use cedar, eucalyptus, fir, pine or spruce chips as they produce an unpleasantly bitter smoke.)

For a more delicate smoke flavor, add dry, unsoaked chips to glowing coals. Chips made from the white oak barrels in which Jack Daniels whiskey is aged are also available (see "Standard Charcoal Briquets," page 10 for information on how to order).

Charcoal Starters

There are several types of charcoal starters on the market.

Liquid Starters

These are the most popular way to start charcoal fires in this country. Devotees claim they are fast, easy and foolproof. Critics claim the lighter-fluid, paint-thinner odors do not dissipate during cooking and are transferred to the food.

To Use: Arrange the briquets in a pyramid on the rack in the bottom of the grill. The pyramid shape allows air to circulate around the coals, which makes them light faster. Saturate the briquets with lighter fluid. Let stand one minute to allow the fluid to permeate. Light the briquets with safety matches in several different places. Do not cover. When the briquets have turned ashen by day, glowing by night, spread them evenly over the rack on the bottom of the grill.

Chimneys

Chimneys are made of galvanized steel or other similarly durable materials, but they resemble large tin cans with heatproof handles and holes for ventilation in the bottom. They work on the draft-furnace principle: papers in the bottom are ignited and the fire is coaxed upward through the charcoal.

To Use: Crumple some newspaper and place it in the bottom of the chimney. Stack the briquets on top of the paper and light the paper through the holes at the chimney bottom. As soon as the briquets are blazing, pour them onto the rack at the bottom of the grill and spread them out in an even layer. If you are using the Indirect Grilling Method, a chimney starter will allow the briquets to be poured easily onto either side of the drip pan. (See "Indirect Grilling Method," page 17.)

Self-Starting Briquets

These are standard charcoal briquets that have been saturated with liquid starter. As noted, many people insist that the chemical odors do not dissipate during cooking and are transferred to the food.

To Use: Spread the briquets out in a single layer on the rack at the bottom of the grill. They should be so close that they touch. Use a long-handled safety match to light them on the edges in several places. Do not cover the grill. Wait until the briquets are ashen by day or glowing by night, then spread them out in an even layer.

Solid Starters

Quick fire starters come as blocks, squares, sticks or rounds of pressed wood fibers impregnated with flammable substances, which cause them to light quickly. These substances burn without a chemical odor, however, so that odd tastes are not added to the food.

To Use: Build a pyramid of briquets in the center of the rack on the grill bottom. Place solid starting blocks in several places on the edges of the pyramid. Light the blocks with long-handled safety matches. The blocks will burn for several minutes, lighting the charcoal in the process. When the coals are ashen, spread them out on the rack in an even layer.

Electric Starters

These oval-shaped electric elements look like they have been taken from your electric broiler. Attached to heatproof handles, they have a long electric cord that plugs into a three-pronged outlet and are virtually foolproof.

To Use: Arrange the briquets in a single layer to cover the bottom of the grill. Place the starter over the charcoal layer, directly in the center of the rack. Heap additional briquets over the starter—enough to bury it. Plug the starter into a three-pronged outlet or use an extension cord. Do not cover the grill. In minutes the starter and surrounding charcoal will be glowing red hot. Remove the starter, unplug it and set it on a heatproof surface until cool. Use a long-handled barbecue fork or similar tool to distribute the glowing briquets evenly over the rack on the grill bottom. Push the cold briquets on the edges of the rack closer to the glowing briquets so they will catch fire, too.

Grilling Equipment and Utensils

There are so many grilling accessories on the market that new grill owners could easily be bewildered by it all. The truth is, only a few basic tools are necessary. These include a wire brush to clean the grid, a long-handled spatula and tongs to turn the food, some oven mitts—the kind that go up to your elbows so you don't burn yourself—and a long-handled basting brush with soft bristles.

Don't invest in a long-handled fork; when you pierce food with a fork to transfer it to or from the grill or to turn it the holes cause valuable juices to run out.

If possible, buy tools with holes cut in the handles, so you can hang them up. Don't buy tools with wooden handles as they scorch very quickly.

You will also need skewers. Metal skewers are available in all sizes, from six inches to 14 inches or longer. A set of six, each 12 or 14 inches, will do fine for most recipes. Food stays in place on a metal skewer more easily if the surface is not completely round and smooth, but has some flat surfaces like a hexagon.

We prefer disposable wooden barbecue skewers, available at Oriental shops (see page 182 for a list of mail-order sources). Not only do they make a more charming presentation, but the natural wood surface is abrasive and holds food in place. Wooden skewers are also available in several sizes. Their only drawback is that they must be soaked in water for 30 minutes to prevent scorching.

We also recommend buying a barbecue basket with a narrow grid. A basket holds several pieces of food and also accommodates small butterflied birds, making it easy to turn them.

Besides the essential equipment, you will need heavy-duty aluminum foil for lining the grill, a bowl of water to sprinkle onto flare-ups and some paper towels and vegetable oil to coat the grid before using.

You may also want to invest in a stainless steel close-meshed cooking tray called a Griffo-grill. It fits directly on the grid and allows juices to drip through, but offers support for the food. Chicken livers, for example, can be placed on this tray without skewers. These grills are sold in supermarkets and food specialty stores. Or write to: Griffo-grill, 301 Oak Street, Quincy, IL 62301.

Cooking on the Grill

Direct Grilling Method

In direct heat grilling, the hot coals are placed directly underneath the food, so the food must be watched carefully, turned often and brushed regularly with marinade so it does not burn or dry out. This is especially true if you are grilling uncovered, since the presence of so much oxygen make the coals burn brightly. Flare-ups are less common when you cover the grill.

The coals can also be arranged so that you have two different degrees of heat. On one part of the grill, spread 75 percent of the hot briquets out in a single layer with just a little space between each; they should not be touching and should cover the same surface as the food. Arrange the remaining 25 percent on the other part of the grill in a small mound; the mound will burn hotter and more intensely and you can use either area as needed.

When grilling with direct heat, remember to watch the food carefully. If your thick piece of poultry is charring on the outside but still raw on the inside, place it on the outer edges of the grid as far from the hottest coals as possible.

Indirect Grilling Method

Only covered grills can be used for this cooking method. In indirect heat grilling, ashen coals are arranged in banks—two to three briquets high—on either side of a dripping pan (any metal baking pan slightly larger than the food placed above it).

There are two ways to prepare the coals. You can make a pyramid, light it, then divide the ashen coals in half, pushing one half to each side of the grill and then place a dripping pan between the two banks. Or you can arrange two banks of coals on either side of the dripping pan and light both sides. We suggest using between 20 and 25 on each side to start.

The food should be positioned directly over the dripping pan so that the juices and rendered fat will not fall into the fire and cause flare-ups. When the coals become ashen, fill the dripping pan half full with water. The constant evaporation helps keep the food moist as it cooks. The grill is covered, and food cooks slowly and doesn't need to be watched constantly. Be prepared, though, to add five or six extra briquets to each side every 30 to 45 minutes, since indirect grilling is a long, slow process.

If you want, you can make your own drip pan out of a double layer of heavy-duty foil with the edges turned up about 2 inches high. Foil pans are also commercially available.

Some cooks like to throw dry or soaked wood chips or other aromatics like herbs onto the ashen coals during indirect cooking, which adds an even smokier flavor.

Water Smoking

Many people don't water smoke because they think it is too hard and takes too long. This is because they confuse it with true smoking and brining—a process that takes place in a smokehouse. Water smoking, which is done in a miniature, portable smoker, is easy to do and usually takes no more than a couple of hours. It is not necessary to use liquid brines or dry seasoning mixtures or to otherwise prepare poultry for smoking. You may want to add a marinade—and we have included several—but this also is not essential.

Once the charcoal is lit, the water pan filled and the food in place on the grid, all the cook has to do is replenish the charcoal every 30 to 45 minutes or so, checking each time to see if more liquid is needed in the water pan. The food does not need to be turned.

A water smoker cooks through a combination of hot air, hot smoke and hot steam, which keeps the food moist by evaporating throughout the cooking process.

For extra smoky flavor, throw handfuls of water-soaked wood chips onto the burning charcoal in your smoker. Do this sparingly, however, or you will end up with food too strongly flavored with smoke.

Spit Roasting (Rotisserie)

Spit roasting can be done over direct or indirect heat and on a covered or uncovered grill. It works wonderfully with whole poultry, from tiny quail to large turkeys, as the circular motion continually bastes the birds. Be sure to position a drip pan directly under the place where the bird drips as it turns, usually at the part just beginning the upswing. Run the spit through the center of the bird and fasten spit forks carefully to keep it in place. Tie the legs and wings close to the body. Spit cooking can be done anywhere from five to ten inches above the fire. When spit cooking heavy birds, such as large turkeys, you may want to use a balance weight. After spitting the birds in place, check the way they turn. If they roll around the spit and do not turn evenly, start over and respit the bird. Otherwise you will end up with a bird cooked well on one side and raw on the other. One of the advantages of spit cooking is that most birds (except for the fattiest ones, like goose) do not have to be watched continually. All you need to do is replenish the charcoal (and water if you are using it) as needed.

How Hot Is Hot Enough?

Once the coals are lit, they must go through three stages to reach the ashen stage perfect for grilling. In the first stage, the coals are aflame and literally burning. Next, they have cooled down slightly and are glowing red, but no longer on fire. Finally, they are covered with a medium-thick layer of gray ash.

Once the coals are ashen, you can use a primitive method to test for correct grilling temperature if you have a five- to six-inch distance between the coals and the grid. Hold one hand, palm down, about $1/2$ inch from the grid. If you can hold your hand there for two seconds, the coals are too hot; three seconds means they are medium-hot, but too hot to grill; four or five seconds means they are medium, which is perfect for either indirect or direct grilling.

When the coals are too hot, partially close the dampers and spread the coals out toward the edges of the grill or remove a few hot coals.

When the coals are not hot enough, open the vents wider and add additional briquets or push the hot coals closer together.

Marinating

Marinades can add flavor to bland poultry or piquancy to rich-flavored fowl; they can lubricate dry fowl, too, since a little oil seeps into the

TURNSPITS Today's rotisserie is based on the medieval turnspit, which was turned by hand and played several songs over and over as a kind of musical timer. After a chef had worked for a particular house for several months, his ear became so attuned to the melodies of the turnspit that he was able to determine the degree of doneness in the food. A roast goose with bread stuffing, for example, might still be running pink juices when the 14th tune— "Greensleeves"— was played, but would be grilled to a crisp turn by the time "God Save the King" was half over.

pores, but marinades cannot effectively tenderize tough meat.

Certain substances such as vinegar, wine, lemon, lime, apple, orange and other fruit juices break down fibers on the surface of the poultry, but not on the inside. Vinegar (except Japanese rice vinegar) is by far the strongest of all of these, and it does not really have a delicious flavor of its own, so we don't recommend vinegar when marinating poultry.

Increasing marinating time will not make the poultry more tender; instead the outside will get mushy while the interior remains unaffected. We have found that 1 hour at room temperature or 2 hours in the refrigerator is sufficient time for marinating poultry. Within this time, the acid breaks down the outside fiber just enough to allow the oil to seep in a little more deeply than it would have without the marinade.

Because of the danger of bacteria, don't let food sit in a marinade for longer than 1 hour at room temperature; if you want to marinate something for 2 or 3 hours, cover it well and put it in the refrigerator.

Do not poke holes in the poultry before marinating. The loss of the vital juices seeping out of the holes is not worth the flavor that creeps in from the marinade.

The marinades in this book were developed to enhance flavor and lubrication, using only those liquids that contain light acids (fruit juice, wine and Japanese rice vinegar) in a 50/50 proportion to oil.

To marinate lean birds, decrease the amount or strength of the acid or add more oil. For fatty birds, increase the amount of acid liquid and decrease the amount of oil. (Basic marinade recipes follow.)

Flavorings and aromatics, such as the following, can be added to your marinade if desired:

- Complementary dried herbs and spices or fresh herbs
- Pungencies like garlic, scallions, onions, leeks, shallots, chives or garlic stems
- Piquancies like fresh or dried hot chilies, hot mustard, black or white pepper

Three Marinades

You need marinate poultry only for an hour (or two in the refrigerator). Don't forget to baste lean poultry with marinade each time you turn it.

BASIC MARINADE   MAKES 1½ CUPS

¾ cup vegetable oil
¾ cup dry red or white wine
1 clove garlic, minced
  Pinch freshly ground black pepper
⅓ cup chopped, stemmed fresh parsley

Combine all of the ingredients and mix well.

MARINADE FOR LEAN BIRDS   MAKES 1½ CUPS

14 tablespoons vegetable oil
½ cup apple cider
1 tablespoon cider vinegar
1 tablespoon water
¼ teaspoon crumbled dried rosemary
¼ teaspoon crumbled dried thyme
¼ teaspoon black freshly ground pepper
2 tablespoons minced fresh chives

Combine all of the ingredients and mix well.

MARINADE FOR FATTY BIRDS   MAKES 1⅔ CUPS

⅓ cup vegetable oil
½ cup fresh orange juice
½ cup apple cider
3 tablespoons fresh lime juice
2 scallions, finely minced
2 bay leaves, crumbled
½ teaspoon red pepper flakes
⅛ teaspoon ground mace

Combine all of the ingredients and mix well.

"What is sauce for the goose may be sauce for the gander. But it is not necessarily sauce for the chicken, the duck, the turkey or the guinea hen."
—Alice B. Toklas, in *The Alice B. Toklas Cookbook*

Taste, Texture and Weight Chart

Domestic Fowl	
Broiler/Fryer	white breast, dark legs and some dark meat; mild flavor; slightly fatty; tender texture; 2 to 3½ pounds
Capon	white breast, dark legs and some dark meat; mild flavor; slightly fattier than broiler/fryer; tender, meaty texture; 6 to 9 pounds
Cornish hen	white breast, dark legs and some dark meat; bland flavor; very slightly fatty; tender texture; 1 to 1½ pounds
Duck	all dark meat; rich flavor; very fatty, but meat is lean; medium-tender texture; 4 to 5 pounds
Free-range chicken	white breast, dark legs and some dark meat; rich, old-fashioned flavor; very slightly fatty; tender texture; 1½ to 3½ pounds
Goose	all dark meat; very rich flavor; very, very fatty, but meat is lean; slightly chewy texture; 9 to 13 pounds; of the many types, the Emit is recommended for use in this book
Poussin (baby chicken)	all white meat; ultradelicate flavor (some say tasteless); fat-free; very tender, juicy texture; 12 to 18 ounces
Turkey	white breast, dark legs and some dark meat; medium-strong flavor; very little fat; tender to very slightly chewy texture; 10 to 26 pounds
Turkey (free-range)	all dark meat; very flavorful; very lean; chewy texture; 8 to 12 pounds

Farm-Raised Tame Game	
Guinea hen	slightly dark, gold-colored meat; flavorful and similar to pheasant; lean and firm; chewy, slightly stringy texture; 2 to 2½ pounds (at 3 pounds they are tough)
Mallard	all dark meat; flavorful taste; lean meat; chewy texture, but more tender than wild duck; 2 to 2½ pounds
Partridge	light-colored meat, similar to baby pheasant; flavorful taste; lean meat; tender, slightly stringy texture; 14 to 16 ounces
Pheasant	off-white breast meat with dark legs; savory taste; lean meat; slightly firm texture, but legs are slightly stringy with tendons; 2 to 2½ pounds or at 1 pound as lighter, more tender baby pheasants; similar in taste to guinea hen
Quail	dark meat (the color of a walnut); delicate but flavorful; very lean; slightly firm texture; 3 to 6 ounces
Squab	reddish brown flesh; rich flavor; lean meat but some fat under the skin; firm, substantial texture; 14 to 17 ounces

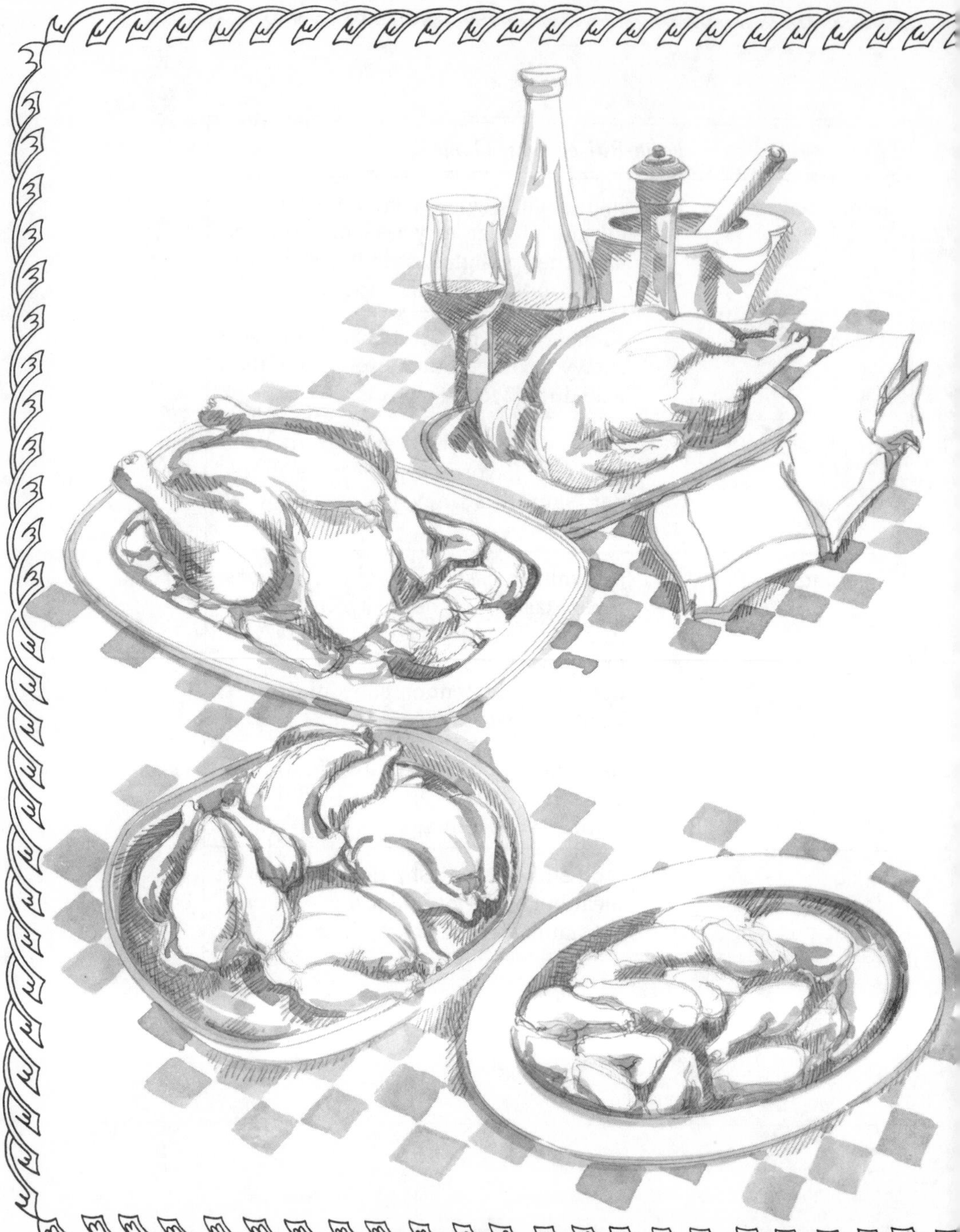

Birds of a Feather

Chicken, Capon and Cornish Hen

Chicken, capon and Cornish hen are eaten in almost every country in the world. They are the oldest domesticated food animals, feeding beggars and aristocrats, armies and artists, children, lovers and kings.

These fowl have been combined with every imaginable flavoring—from soy sauce in Japan, to oregano in Greece, to barbecue sauce in the United States.

In this book we have used these flavorings plus others that we feel will bring pleasure to your dining companions.

Perfect Grilled Chicken with Five Sauces

SERVES 4

These five sauces provide a unique "wardrobe" for a perfect grilled chicken. Each sauce complements the chicken in a different way and would be appropriate for any occasion. All the sauces can be made while the chicken grills.

1   **whole fresh chicken, about 3 pounds**
1   **recipe Basic Marinade (see page 21)**
2   **cups hickory chips**

1. Removing any visible fat, put the chicken and marinade into a large ziplock plastic bag, seal the bag and turn it several times to coat the chicken. Place the bag in a large bowl and let sit at room temperature for 1 hour (or 2 hours in the refrigerator), turning several times.

2. Soak the hickory chips in water to cover 30 minutes or longer. Prepare the grill for the Indirect Grilling Method (see page 17). Light the coals. When the briquets are ashen, remove the chicken from the marinade. Drain the hickory chips and scatter them over the hot coals.

3. Place the chicken, breast side up, on an ungreased grid over the dripping pan. Grill, covered, over indirect heat for 1 hour, checking after 30 minutes to see if the coals need replenishing. To test for doneness, insert a fork into the deepest part of the thigh. If the juices run clear and the joints move easily, the chicken is done. If the juices run pink, the chicken needs more grilling.

4. Remove the chicken from the grill and let sit for 15 minutes at room temperature before carving. Serve with any of the following sauces.

TO COOK INDOORS: Place the chicken on a rack in a roasting pan filled with ¼ inch of water. Cook at 375 degrees for 1 hour. After 30 minutes, baste with the remaining marinade. Serve as above.

A King-Sized Bed of Hot Green Salsa

MAKES 3 CUPS

Cilantro (fresh coriander) is an aromatic green herb resembling fresh parsley, only with flatter leaves. It is available in Hispanic food markets.

4   4-ounce cans mild green chili peppers, drained and coarsely chopped
6   scallions, cut into 1-inch lengths
4   cloves garlic, peeled and halved
4–6 fresh jalapeño peppers, to taste
1   cup fresh cilantro (or substitute fresh parsley)
1   cup virgin olive oil

1   Perfect Grilled Chicken (see page 28)

1. Place the chili peppers in a food processor fitted with the steel blade along with the scallions and garlic halves. Split the jalapeño peppers lengthwise, remove the seeds (wear rubber gloves to do this if possible) and add to the food processor along with the cilantro and olive oil. Pulse several times until coarsely chopped. Do not puree.

2. Spoon the salsa onto a serving platter large enough to hold the chicken. Arrange in a bed or nest and place the grilled chicken in the center. Carve at the table, spooning a helping of salsa onto each dinner plate alongside each serving of hot chicken.

Vidalia Soubise Sauce

MAKES 3 CUPS

In this recipe, our perfect chicken is grilled with a layer of Vidalia onion slices inserted under the skin and served with a classic French Soubise (onion) sauce, which is also made with this sweet, mild onion from Vidalia, Georgia. If Vidalia onions are not available, substitute any sweet, mild onion.

1   Perfect Grilled Chicken (see page 28), prepared through Step 2
½   cup chopped fresh parsley
1   Vidalia onion; thinly sliced

VIDALIA SOUBISE SAUCE

3   **cups half-and-half**

3   **large Vidalia onions, thinly sliced**

¼   **cup unsalted butter**

¼   **cup all-purpose flour**

¼   **teaspoon salt**

⅛   **teaspoon ground mace**

⅛   **teaspoon freshly ground white pepper**

1. Place the chicken on the counter with the cavity facing you. Take off any rings or bracelets; you are going to loosen the skin from the breast meat on both sides of the breastbone. Open a pocket on one side of the breastbone using your fingers. Work deeper and deeper, enlarging the pocket until your whole hand is inside. Although the skin is fastened tightly to the breastbone and at the bottom of the drumstick, you will still be able to make a large pocket at the thigh and down slightly past the top of the drumstick. Make a pocket on the other side of the breastbone in the same way.

2. Scatter the parsley on a large dinner plate and dip the onion slices in it to partially coat. Insert onion slices into the chicken pockets until the skin and flesh are not touching at any point on the breast. If the onion slices start to fall out, use small wooden skewers or round wooden toothpicks to close the edges of the skin. Grill the chicken as directed in Steps 3 and 4 (see page 28).

3. While the chicken grills, prepare the Vidalia Soubise: Pour the half-and-half into large saucepan, add the sliced onions and simmer over low heat for 8 to 10 minutes, until the onions are tender. Allow the mixture to cool slightly. Transfer it to a food processor fitted with the steel blade and puree onions coarsely.

4. Heat the butter in a large saucepan until sizzling and stir in the flour with a wire whisk. Cook over low heat for 3 to 4 minutes, stirring constantly, while the mixture bubbles. Stir in the salt, mace and pepper, mixing well.

5. Strain the sauce, discarding the solids, and return it to the pan. Transfer to a serving bowl and spoon over the hot chicken slices.

Apricot-Cranberry Sauce

MAKES 1¾ CUPS

APRICOT-CRANBERRY SAUCE

6   ounces dried apricots

1   cup fresh orange juice

1   tablespoon grated orange zest

¼   cup chicken broth

3   tablespoons orange liqueur, such as Triple Sec or Grand Marnier

1   teaspoon ground cinnamon

¼   teaspoon freshly grated nutmeg

2   tablespoons brown sugar

½   cup canned cranberry sauce

1   Perfect Grilled Chicken (see page 28)

1. Place the apricots in a medium-sized saucepan and add just enough water to cover. Bring to a boil, reduce the heat and cook over medium heat until tender, about 10 minutes. Transfer the apricots with any remaining liquid to a food processor fitted with the steel blade and puree.

2. Add the orange juice, orange zest, chicken broth, orange liqueur, cinnamon, nutmeg and brown sugar. Pulse until well combined.

3. Spoon the mixture into a serving bowl and stir in the cranberry sauce. Serve at room temperature with hot grilled chicken slices.

Delicious Five-Minute Caviar Sauce

MAKES 2 CUPS

This recipe should not be made with expensive Russian caviar. American whitefish caviar makes an excellent sauce. If it's not available in your area, see page 182 for our list of mail-order sources.

2   cups sour cream or sour half-and-half
2   scallions, minced
½   teaspoon dried thyme
2   ounces American whitefish caviar

1   Perfect Grilled Chicken (see page 28)

1. Combine the sour cream, minced scallions and thyme in a small bowl and divide evenly among 4 individual shallow sauce dishes, such as butter chips. Cover each dish with plastic wrap and refrigerate.

2. At serving time, drizzle the caviar evenly over the sour cream in each small dish and bring to the table with Perfect Grilled Chicken on a platter. Guests should spoon the caviar sauce over the hot chicken slices.

Two Butters in Crocks

MAKES: 1 CUP SHERRY-ALMOND BUTTER
¾ CUP PORT-WALNUT BUTTER

These butters can be made well in advance if covered and refrigerated. If you don't wish to serve them in crocks, form each into a roll the diameter of a quarter and wrap in plastic wrap. Thirty minutes before serving, remove the plastic wrap and place the rolls on a small rectangular or oval platter to allow them to come to room temperature. Sprinkle a little chopped parsley over the rolls, if desired.

SHERRY-ALMOND BUTTER
½   cup (1 stick) unsalted butter, at room temperature
3   tablespoons dry sherry
½   cup ground almonds
¼   teaspoon freshly grated nutmeg

PORT-WALNUT BUTTER

¹⁄₂   **cup (1 stick) unsalted butter, at room temperature**

¹⁄₄   **cup port**

¹⁄₃   **cup ground walnuts**

2   **tablespoons finely minced fresh parsley**

1   **tablespoon fresh minced parsley for sprinkling on butters**

1   **Perfect Grilled Chicken (see page 28)**

1. Prepare the Sherry-Almond Butter: Combine the butter, sherry, almonds and nutmeg in a bowl and stir to mix well. Transfer to a crock, cover and refrigerate.

2. Prepare the Port-Walnut Butter: Combine the butter, port, walnuts and 2 tablespoons minced parsley in a bowl and stir to mix well. Transfer to a crock, cover and refrigerate.

3. Thirty minutes before serving, bring the crocks to the table and sprinkle each with ¹⁄₂ tablespoon chopped parsley. Allow the butters to come to room temperature. Bring the chicken to the table on a serving platter and carve. Guests should spread the butters onto the hot chicken slices.

Transylvanian Grilled Chicken

SERVES 6

This recipe is based on a Transylvanian roast chicken recipe, which may be similar to one served by Count Dracula himself in Bram Stoker's novel, *Dracula*. The count served some cheese, a salad, a hot bird and a cold bottle of wine to his young guest, Jonathan Harker, who ate with enthusiasm, while Dracula, saving room for later, didn't touch a drop.

Here the recipe has been adapted for the grill and a marinade has been added to give the chicken extra succulence. Garlic (long rumored to be a surefire remedy to ward off vampires) has been added, too. Transylvanians are crazy about *mujdei*—a fresh roasted garlic sauce that they spread on their roast chicken. You can easily achieve the same effect if you grill unpeeled garlic cloves on the outer edges of a grid for 20 minutes. Press the cloves gently to squeeze out the soft garlic and spread it onto the pieces of hot grilled chicken.

And why not add a salad and cheese to the menu like the count? Toss bibb and romaine leaves together with a tart vinaigrette dressing and some heated French bread; spread with mild goat cheese. Add a cold bottle of Transylvanian wine such as Premiat or Tranave Castle Riesling and the setting will be complete.

If elephant garlic or wooden skewers aren't available in your area, see page 182 for mail-order sources.

2   **chickens, about 3 pounds each**

MARINADE
1   **cup olive oil**
¹/₂   **cup fresh lemon juice**
2   **small onions, quartered**
³/₄   **teaspoon paprika**
¹/₂   **teaspoon freshly ground pepper**

6   **wooden skewers, soaked in water for 30 minutes before use**
12   **cloves elephant garlic, unpeeled**
4   **red bell peppers, seeded and cut into strips lengthwise**

2   cups sour cream in serving bowl sprinkled with 2 teaspoons
    paprika for garnish

1. Wash and dry the chickens. Cut each one into 12 pieces using poultry shears or a Chinese cleaver (or ask your butcher to do it): Cut
   chickens in half lengthwise and remove the wings and legs. Cut
   each half into 4 pieces of equal width. Put 12 pieces in 1 large plastic
   ziplock bag and 12 in another.

2. Prepare the marinade: Combine the olive oil, lemon juice, onions,
   paprika and black pepper in a food processor fitted with the steel
   blade and pulse until coarsely pureed.

3. Divide the marinade between the 2 bags. Seal the bags and turn
   several times to coat the chicken. Put each bag in a bowl and let sit at
   room temperature for 1 hour (or 2 hours in the refrigerator), turning
   the bag several times.

4. Drain the skewers. Put 2 unpeeled cloves of elephant garlic on each
   skewer.

5. Prepare the grill for the Direct Grilling Method (see page 16). Light
   the coals. When the briquets become ashen, remove the chicken
   from the marinade, reserving the marinade. Place chicken pieces on
   oiled grid over ashen coals and cook, covered, over direct heat for 24
   minutes, turning every 6 minutes and brushing with marinade each
   time. Wings will need to be turned every 3 minutes.

6. Brush the pepper strips with marinade and place them on the grid
   with the chicken, skin side down. Grill for 5 minutes or until they
   begin to char. Keep the pepper strips warm on the outer edges of the
   grid (or in a 250-degree oven on a heatproof dish if the grid is
   crowded).

7. Place the garlic skewers on the edges of the grid and grill for 15
   minutes, turning every 5 minutes. When the garlic is soft enough to
   squeeze out of its skin, transfer garlic to a large serving platter.

8. Transfer the chicken to a serving platter and bring to the table with
   the garlic skewers, pepper strips and the bowl of sour cream sprinkled with paprika. Each guest helps himself to chicken and
   squeezes the garlic cloves onto the chicken pieces.

TO COOK INDOORS: Arrange the chicken on a foil-lined cookie

sheet and bake in a 375-degree oven for 45–55 minutes until the juices run clear when the meat is pricked with a fork. Brush with marinade after 15 minutes. When the chicken has been in the oven 30 minutes, add the garlic cloves (unskewered). Remove the chicken and garlic and set aside. Sauté the pepper strips in 3 teaspoons olive oil for 5 minutes. Bring everything to the table as directed.

Grilled Free-Range Chicken with Mace Sauce and Bread Stuffing

SERVES 4 TO 6

1   free-range chicken, about 3½ pounds, with giblets

STUFFING

3   slices day-old bread, crusts removed, cut into ½-inch cubes
½   cup milk
1   teaspoon dried thyme
3   tablespoons minced fresh parsley
1   clove garlic, minced
¼   teaspoon ground mace
¼   teaspoon salt
½   teaspoon freshly ground pepper

1   medium carrot, unpeeled, cut into ½-inch chunks
1   stalk celery, cut into ½-inch chunks
2   tablespoons vegetable oil
¼   cup whole cloves

MACE SAUCE

8   peppercorns
8   whole cloves
2   small onions, peeled
2   cups milk
2   small bay leaves

¼   teaspoon ground mace

1¼ cups breadcrumbs
1   tablespoon unsalted butter
¼   cup half-and-half
     Parsley sprigs for garnish (optional)

1. Wash and dry the chicken and arrange it breast side up on the counter with the cavity facing you. Take off any rings or bracelets. You will be loosening the skin from the breast meat on both sides of the breastbone. Carefully, without tearing the skin, open a pocket on one side of the breastbone using your fingers. Work deeper and deeper, enlarging the pocket until your whole hand is inside. Although the skin is fastened tightly to the breastbone and fastened at the bottom of the drumstick, you will still be able to make a large pocket at the thigh and down slightly past the top of the drumstick. Make a pocket on the other side of the breastbone in the same way.

2. Prepare the stuffing: Simmer the giblets in water to cover in a small saucepan for 10 minutes or until tender. Drain, cool and mince. In a large bowl combine the minced giblets with the bread cubes, milk, thyme, parsley, garlic, mace, salt and pepper, mixing well.

3. Divide the stuffing into 2 parts to fill the pockets, pushing the stuffing down to the drumstick on each side. Put the carrot and celery chunks inside the chicken's cavity. Brush the whole chicken with the vegetable oil.

4. Prepare the grill for the Indirect Grilling Method (see page 17). Light the coals. When the briquets become ashen, add the cloves to the water in the pan as an aromatic.

5. Place the chicken on an oiled grid, breast side up, over the dripping pan. Open the dampers slightly. Grill, covered, over indirect heat for 70 minutes without turning, checking after 30 or 45 minutes to see whether the water has evaporated or more coals are needed. At the same time, check for hot spots—if the chicken is cooking too quickly in any one place, rotate it slightly.

6. When the chicken has 30 minutes left to grill, prepare the Mace Sauce: Crush the peppercorns in a mortar with a pestle or put them in a dishtowel and crush with a rolling pin. Place the pepper in a medium-sized saucepan. Stick 4 cloves into each onion and add the

onions to the saucepan along with the milk, bay leaves and mace. Bring to a boil, transfer the pan to a cool surface and let stand for 20 minutes at room temperature, uncovered.

7. Check the chicken for doneness by inserting a fork into the thigh; if the juices run clear, it is done; if they run pink, the chicken needs more time on the grill. Carefully remove the chicken from the grill and discard celery and carrot chunks. Let stand for 10 minutes.

8. Disjoint the legs and place the chicken on a serving platter. Remove the breast sections on each side of the breastbone, cutting carefully along the breastbone and easing the knife underneath the meat so it can be removed in one piece. Cut each breast into 4 or 5 slices.

9. Strain the sauce and pour it back into the saucepan, add the bread-crumbs and bring to a boil over medium heat. Add the butter and half-and-half. Pour the sauce into a large, dark-colored oval platter so that it just barely covers the bottom. Arrange the legs and breast slices over the sauce. Garnish with the parsley sprigs, if desired.

TO COOK INDOORS: Prepare chicken as for grilling. Place the chicken on oiled rack, uncovered, in a roasting pan. Roast for 70 minutes at 375 degrees. Let stand 10 minutes before slicing.

Tom Jones's Capon

SERVES 8 TO 10

In the movie *Tom Jones*, starring Albert Finney, protagonist Jones shares a seductive dinner in an 18th-century tavern with an older woman named Jenny Waters. No words are spoken, but the characters let the audience know exactly what they are thinking as they eat the whole meal very suggestively with their hands. If you want to duplicate their menu, include a glass of sherry and a tankard of ale.

This grilled capon is close to what an 18th-century capon—roasted in a wood burning oven—must have tasted like. We've added a pear, rose-mary and breadcrumb stuffing. You may want to have cold asparagus stalks with a vinaigrette dipping sauce alongside, since these can be eaten with your hands, 18th-century style.

1   large, fresh capon, about 7 pounds

MARINADE

½   cup virgin olive oil

¼   cup fresh, strained lemon juice

½   teaspon crumbled dried rosemary

STUFFING

1½   cups packed fresh breadcrumbs

2   medium-sized pears, peeled, cored and coarsely chopped (about 1 cup)

2   tablespoons sugar

⅛   teaspoon freshly grated nutmeg

⅛   teaspoon dried rosemary

4   tablespoons unsalted butter

1   onion, quartered

1   celery stalk, cut into ½-inch chunks

1   carrot, unpeeled, cut into ½ chunks

1. Wash and dry the capon and put it in a large ziplock plastic bag.

2. Prepare the marinade: Combine the oil, lemon juice and rosemary in a small bowl. Pour the marinade into bag. Seal the bag and turn several times. Put the bag in a large bowl and marinate at room temperature for 1 hour (or 2 hours in the refrigerator), turning several times.

3. Remove the capon from the marinade, reserving marinade. Place it, breast side up, on the counter with the cavity facing you. Take off any rings or bracelets. You are going to loosen the skin from the breast meat on both sides of the breastbone. Carefully, without tearing the skin, open a pocket on one side of the breastbone, using your fingers. Work deeper and deeper, enlarging the pocket until your whole hand is inside. Although the skin is fastened tightly to the breastbone and at the bottom of the drumstick, you will still be able to make a large pocket at the thigh and down slightly past the top of the drumstick. Make a pocket on the other side of the breastbone in the same way.

MEDIEVAL CAPON
WITH ROSE PETALS
AND ALMONDS:
"Take the flowris of rosys and wash hem well in water, and thenne take almonds and temper hem and seethe hem and take flesh of capons and hack it small and then gray (grind) hem well in a mortar and thenne do it in the rose so that the flesh accord with the milk and so that the meat be chargeaunt; and after do it fire to boyle and do thereto sugar and saffron and it be well coloured and rosy of leaves."
—From *The Form of Cury*, a 1390 cookbook commissioned by King Richard II

4. Prepare the stuffing: Combine the breadcrumbs, pears, sugar, nut-meg, rosemary and butter in a small bowl. Divide the stuffing into 2 parts and fill the pockets, pushing the stuffing all the way into the pockets, down to the drumsticks. Place onion quarters, celery and carrot chunks inside the chicken cavity.

5. Prepare the grill for the Indirect Grilling Method (see page 17). Light the coals, and when the briquets become ashen, place the capon on an oiled grid, breast side up. Grill, covered, over indirect heat for 3 hours without turning, checking every 30 to 45 minutes to see if more water or coals are needed. Baste the bird with the reserved marinade each time you lift the cover.

6. Check for doneness by inserting a fork into the thigh; if the juices run clear, it is done; if they run pink, the capon needs more time on the grill.

7. Carefully remove the capon from the grill and discard the onion quarters, celery and carrot chunks. Transfer the bird to a serving platter, let stand for 10 minutes, bring it to the table and carve.

TO COOK INDOORS: Place the capon on an oiled rack, uncovered, in a roasting pan. Roast for 2 hours at 375 degrees. Let stand for 10 minutes before carving.

Barbecued Chicken in a Garlic Bread Basket

SERVES 4 TO 6

This basket is easily carved out of a large, round Italian bread loaf, which is brushed with garlic butter and heated. When hot, it is filled with the barbecued chicken pieces. Diners should tear off pieces of the basket to eat with the chicken. We use one 3-pound chicken for six people. If your guests are big eaters, you may want to grill more. The barbecue sauce can be doubled.

BARBECUE SAUCE

1	tablespoon safflower oil
1	large leek (white part only), sliced
2	cloves garlic, minced
1	cup canned tomatoes, with liquid
³/₄	cup ketchup
¹/₂	cup brown sugar
¹/₄	cup cider vinegar
3	tablespoons dark molasses
2	teaspoons Dijon mustard
2	teaspoons chili powder
¹/₄	teaspoon salt
¹/₄	teaspoon freshly ground pepper

This delicious barbecue sauce can be refrigerated or frozen and will make a wonderful hostess gift. If it thickens in the refrigerator, stir in a little water with a wire whisk as you reheat it.

CHICKEN

1	chicken, about 3 pounds
1	round Italian bread loaf, 1¹/₂–2 pounds with a 9-inch diameter
6	tablespoons unsalted butter
2	cloves garlic, minced

1. Prepare the barbecue sauce: Heat the oil in medium-sized saucepan. Add the leeks and garlic and cook, stirring occasionally, until softened, about 3 minutes. Stir in the tomatoes, ketchup, sugar, vinegar, molasses, mustard, chili powder, salt and pepper, mixing well to combine.

2. Bring to a boil, reduce the heat and simmer for 6 to 8 minutes, stirring occasionally. Remove from the heat and reserve.

3. Cut the chicken into 12 pieces using poultry shears or a Chinese cleaver (or ask your butcher to do it): Cut the chicken in half lengthwise and remove the wings and legs. Cut each half into 4 pieces of equal width.

4. Wash and dry the chicken pieces. Brush them liberally on both sides with the barbecue sauce and place them on a glass or ceramic dish in a single layer. Cover with plastic wrap and let sit at room temperature for 1 hour (or 2 hours in the refrigerator), turning occasionally. Leave the unused sauce in the saucepan and set aside.

5. Cut a large circle out of the top of the bread loaf and reserve. Pull the

soft white inside out of the bread to make a bowl and use a small, sharp knife to remove the white inside from the cut-out bread circle (this will be the basket "cover"). Reserve the bread removed from the inside.

6. Melt the butter with the garlic in a small saucepan and let sit for 5 minutes. Brush the inside of the bread basket (including the inside of the cover) with the garlic butter.

7. Prepare the grill for the Direct Grilling Method (see page 16). Light the coals. When the briquets become ashen, arrange the chicken pieces on an oiled grid, skin side up, over the coals. Grill covered, over direct heat for 24 minutes, turning the chicken every 6 minutes and brushing with sauce each time. Wings should be turned every 3 minutes.

8. When the chicken is almost cooked, place the bread basket and cover in a 350-degree oven for 10 to 15 minutes or until lightly toasted. Reheat the reserved sauce.

9. Arrange the chicken pieces in the bread basket, piling them on top of each other. Place the cover over the chicken, surround the basket with reserved bread for dunking and bring to the table along with the reheated sauce in a sauceboat.

TO COOK INDOORS: Arrange the chicken pieces, skin side down, on a foil-lined cookie sheet. Brush them generously with the sauce and bake for 30 minutes at 375 degrees. Turn the pieces, brush again with sauce and cook for 30 minutes more or until done. Serve as directed.

Grilled Cornish Hens
with Fragrant Fruit Sauce

SERVES 6

6   Cornish hens, 16–18 ounces each, all visible fat removed
     Double recipe of Basic Marinade (see page 21).
1   large lemon, cut into 6 wedges
¼   cup whole cloves, soaked briefly in water and drained
1½   cups Fragrant Fruit Sauce (recipe follows)

1. Wash and dry the hens. Place 2 hens in each of 3 ziplock plastic bags. Pour about ¾ cup marinade into each bag. Seal and turn bags several times to coat hens. Place each bag in a separate bowl and marinate at room temperature 1 hour (or 2–3 hours in the refrigerator), turning bags several times.

2. Prepare the grill for the Indirect Grilling Method (see page 17). Light the coals. When the briquets become ashen, sprinkle the drained cloves over them as an aromatic.

3. Remove the hens from the marinade, place 1 lemon wedge in each hen cavity and arrange them on the oiled grid, breast side up, over dripping pan. Grill, covered, over indirect heat for 45 minutes or until the joints move easily and the juices run clear when the hens are pierced with a fork in the thigh.

4. Transfer the hens to a serving platter and bring them to the table. Serve 1 to each guest and pass the Fragrant Fruit Sauce.

TO COOK INDOORS: Arrange the marinated hens, breast side up, on a foil-lined cookie sheet and roast at 325 degrees for 35 minutes or until well browned.

Fragrant Fruit Sauce

MAKES 1½ CUPS

¾   cup port
½   cup cranberry juice
¼   cup cherry jelly, any style
2   tablespoons fresh lemon juice
1   tablespoon grated lemon zest
¼   teaspoon freshly grated nutmeg
¼   teaspoon salt
¼   teaspoon freshly ground pepper

1. Combine all the ingredients in a small saucepan and bring to a boil over medium heat. Reduce heat and simmer 5 minutes or until jelly is dissolved and the sauce is hot. Serve warm or hot with Grilled Cornish Hens.

Chicken Breasts Stuffed with Cornbread and Hot Sausage

SERVES 6

¾   cup hot Italian sausage, (casing removed to measure)

CORNBREAD AND SAUSAGE STUFFING
1¼   cups yellow cornmeal
¾   cup all-purpose flour
¼   cup sugar
2   teaspoons baking powder
½   teaspoon salt
⅛   teaspoon cayenne pepper
1¼   cups milk
¼   cup melted unsalted butter

1   **egg, lightly beaten**

6   **chicken breast halves**

3   **tablespoons olive oil**

1   **tablespoon minced fresh parsley**

1. Crumble the sausage into a frying pan and sauté for 6 minutes over medium heat, until lightly browned. Drain on paper towels, pressing to extract as much fat as possible.

2. In a large mixing bowl, combine the cornmeal, flour, sugar, baking powder, salt and cayenne pepper. Add the milk, melted butter, egg and crumbled sausage, stirring only until the dry ingredients are moistened.

3. Preheat the oven to 400 degrees. Line a 12-cupcake pan with paper liners and fill each ⅔ full with the cornbread mixture. Bake 20 minutes or until golden brown. Remove from the oven and place on a wire rack. Cool for 5 minutes before removing the muffins from the pan. Crumble 3 muffins into a bowl. Arrange the remaining muffins on a serving platter.

4. Prepare the grill for the Direct Grilling Method (see page 16). Light the coals. Wash and dry the chicken breasts. Cut the wings off the chicken and reserve for another use. Remove all visible fat from the chicken. Carefully insert your fingers between the skin and the flesh of each breast, making a large pocket in each. Take care not to tear the skin.

5. Push the cornbread mixture loosely into the pockets with your fingers using about 3 tablespoons in each breast half. Pat the breasts lightly with your hands to flatten and smooth the skin. Brush the skin lightly with olive oil and sprinkle the parsley over the breasts.

6. When the briquets become ashen, arrange the chicken, skin side up, on an oiled grid over the ashen coals and grill, uncovered, for 15 to 20 minutes, turning the breasts every 5 minutes with a long-handled spatula. Transfer the chicken to a serving platter and bring to the table with the platter of muffins.

TO COOK INDOORS: Make the muffins as directed and stuff the chicken breast halves. Brush with oil and sprinkle with parsley. Place the chicken breasts, skin side up, on a rack on a cookie sheet. Bake at 375 degrees for about 15 to 20 minutes or until done. Serve as above.

GOLDEN EGGS There is a breed of South American chickens called Araucañas, meaning "Easter egg chickens," because they lay colored eggs ranging from green to blue to pale pink and sometimes even silver and gold. Yet, despite their beautifully colored exteriors, the eggs taste exactly the same as an ordinary white or brown egg sold in the supermarket.

Grilled Chicken Breasts with Moroccan Stuffing

SERVES 6

MOROCCAN STUFFING
3   cloves garlic, peeled and halved
1   tablespoon ground cumin
¼   teaspoon freshly ground pepper
½   cup fresh parsley without stems
½   cup virgin olive oil
2   cups fresh breadcrumbs

3   whole chicken breasts, halved
¼   cup virgin olive oil

1. Prepare the stuffing: Combine the garlic, cumin, pepper, parsley and ½ cup olive oil in a food processor fitted with the steel blade. Pulse several times to chop finely. Transfer to a bowl and stir in the breadcrumbs, mixing well. Reserve.

2. Wash and dry the breasts, removing any visible fat. Carefully insert your fingers between the skin and the flesh of each breast, making a large pocket in each, taking care not to tear the skin. Spoon 2 to 3 tablespoons of stuffing into each pocket. Smooth the skin back in place. Brush each breast with the ¼ cup olive oil.

3. Prepare the grill for the Direct Grilling Method (see page 16). Light the coals. Place the breasts on an oiled grid, stuffing side up, over the ashen coals. Grill, covered, over direct heat for 18 to 24 minutes, turning each piece every 5 to 6 minutes with long-handled tongs. The breasts are done when the juices run clear if the meat is pricked with a fork.

4. Transfer to a large serving platter, bring to the table and serve immediately.

TO COOK INDOORS: Prepare the breasts with stuffing as directed above. Arrange them on a foil-lined cookie sheet and bake for 35 minutes at 375 degrees. Prick the breasts with a fork as above to test for doneness.

Korean Red Chicken

SERVES 6

This recipe uses a delicious Korean ingredient called *kochu chang*, a dark red soybean and rice puree enlivened with enough red pepper to give it a spicy kick. If you are a hot food lover, you may find yourself spooning it out of the container and eating it as is. The light soy sauce, Oriental sesame oil and hot red bean paste are all available in Korean markets. Or see page 182 for mail-order sources. Do not confuse kochu chang with the red bean paste sold in Japanese markets.

2   chickens, 2½ pounds each

HOT RED BEAN PASTE MARINADE

4   cloves garlic, minced

4   scallions, chopped

1   cup hot red bean paste (kochu chang)

3   tablepoons sugar

3   tablespoons Japanese soy sauce

4   teaspoons Oriental sesame oil

¼   cup water

1. Wash and dry the chickens. Using poultry shears or a Chinese cleaver, cut each chicken into 12 pieces (or ask your butcher to do it): Remove the wings and drumsticks. Cut each chicken in half and then cut each half into 4 pieces of equal width. Place 12 pieces in 1 large ziplock plastic bag and 12 pieces in another.

2. Prepare the Hot Red Bean Paste Marinade: Combine all the marinade ingredients in a small bowl. Mix well, then divide the mixture between the 2 large plastic bags, spooning the marinade over the chicken. Seal the bags and turn them several times, making sure all the pieces are coated with marinade. Put each bag in a large bowl and let sit at room temperature for 1 hour (or 2 hours in the refrigerator), turning often.

3. Prepare the grill for the Direct Grilling Method (see page 16). Light the coals. Place the chicken pieces on an oiled grid over the ashen coals. Grill over direct heat for 24 minutes, turning every 6 minutes and brushing with the reserved marinade each time. Wings should be turned every 3 minutes.

TO COOK INDOORS: Arrange the chicken pieces on a foil-covered cookie sheet and bake at 375 degrees for 45 to 50 minutes or until done. Brush the chicken with the reserved marinade after the first 20 minutes.

Chicken Quarters with Tart Lemon Sauce

A delicious accompaniment to this recipe is Sweet and Sour Potato Packets (recipe follows), which can be prepared and cooked at the same time as the chicken quarters.

SERVES 6 TO 8

2   chickens, about 2½ pounds each, quartered and all visible fat removed
1   recipe Basic Marinade (see page 21)

TART LEMON SAUCE
1   tablespoon cornstarch
3   tablespoons water
½   teaspoon chopped lemon zest
½   teaspoon ground ginger
     Juice of 2 lemons
2   scallions, very finely minced
1   cup water
5   tablespoons light brown sugar
¼   cup chicken broth

     Parsley sprigs for garnish

1. Wash and dry the chicken pieces and divide them evenly between 2 large ziplock plastic bags. Pour half the marinade into one bag and half into the other. Seal each bag and turn to coat the chicken several times. Place the bags on a cookie sheet and let sit at room temperature for 1 hour (or 2 hours in the refrigerator), turning occasionally.

2. Meanwhile, prepare the Tart Lemon Sauce: Combine the cornstarch and 3 tablespoons water in a medium bowl with a wire whisk until no lumps remain. Reserve. Stir together the lemon zest, ginger, lemon juice, scallions and 1 cup water in a saucepan. Add the sugar and chicken broth, stirring well.

3. Bring the mixture to a boil over medium heat, stirring often. Reduce the heat to a simmer. Spoon a few tablespoons of the hot lemon mixture into the cornstarch mixture and combine well until no lumps remain. Spoon a few more tablespoons of the hot lemon mixture into the cornstarch. Then add the cornstarch mixture to the hot lemon sauce. Return to a simmer and cook, stirring often, for 3 to 4 minutes. Let stand in the saucepan until ready to serve.

4. Prepare the grill for the Direct Grilling Method (see page 16). Light the coals. When the briquets become ashen, remove the chicken pieces from the marinade, reserving the marinade. Arrange the chicken on an oiled grid over the ashen coals. Grill, covered, over direct heat for 25 to 30 minutes, turning every 6 minutes and brushing with marinade each time.

5. Reheat the lemon sauce, but do not let it come to a boil. Pour the sauce into a sauceboat and bring it to the table. Arrange the chicken quarters on a serving platter and garnish with the parsley sprigs. Serve hot with the lemon sauce.

TO COOK INDOORS: Place the marinated chicken quarters on a foil-lined cookie sheet. Bake in a 375-degree oven for 40 to 45 minutes, without turning, until golden brown and cooked through. Serve as directed.

Sweet and Sour Potato Packets

SERVES 6

6   round white potatoes, peeled
3   large sweet potatoes, peeled
1   teaspoon salt
18   pitted prunes
6   gingersnaps
2   tablespoons fresh lemon juice
¼   cup brown sugar

1. Cut the white potatoes into quarters to yield 24 pieces. Cut the sweet potatoes in half lengthwise, then cut each half into 4 pieces to yield 24 pieces. Fill a large saucepan with water, add the salt and bring to a boil. Add the potatoes, return to a boil and reduce the heat to a simmer. Simmer for 10 minutes or until just fork-tender. Drain and reserve.

2. Place 6 12-inch-square sheets of foil on the counter. Put 4 pieces of white potato and 4 pieces of sweet potato in the center of each foil sheet. Add 3 prunes to each packet and sprinkle a crumbled ginger-snap over each. Then sprinkle 1 teaspoon lemon juice and 2 teaspoons brown sugar over each packet.

3. Bring the 4 corners of 1 foil packet to the center and twist together to shut. Repeat with the remaining 5 packets.

4. Place each packet on the outer edge of a greased grid over ashen coals. Grill for 15 minutes, rotating the packets every 5 minutes. Transfer to a serving platter and bring to the table. Serve the packets closed, allowing guests to open their own.

TO COOK INDOORS: Arrange the packets on a cookie sheet in a 375-degree oven for 35 minutes. Serve as directed.

Butterflied Cornish Hens with Grilled Papaya

SERVES 6

PAPAYA BASTING SAUCE

2   ripe papaya, peeled, seeded and cut into ½-inch cubes
½   cup fresh orange juice

6   Cornish hens, about 18 ounces each
3   tablespoons brown sugar
4   teaspoons light rum
3   ripe papaya, halved and seeds removed

1. Prepare the Papayas Basting Sauce: Place the papaya cubes in a food processor, fitted with the steel blade and puree. Add the orange juice and pulse to combine.

2. Wash and dry the hens. Butterfly the hens by cutting down the length of the backbone with kitchen scissors or poultry shears. Open the bird to butterfly position on a flat surface. Use the heel of your hand to pound sharply on the breastbone until you hear a crack and the hens lie flat. Brush the hens with the basting sauce.

3. Prepare the grill for the Direct Grilling Method (see page 16). Light the coals. When the coals become ashen, place the butterflied hens, skin side up, on an oiled grid over the ashen coals. Grill, covered, over direct heat for about 20 minutes, turning every 4 minutes with long-handled tongs. Brush the hens twice more with basting sauce as you turn them. The hens are done if the juices run clear when the hen is pricked with a fork

4. Five minutes before the hens are done, mix the sugar and rum together. Brush the cut side of the papaya halves with the sugar-rum mixture. Place the papaya halves on the grid, cut side down, for 1 minute, then turn and grill 2 minutes longer.

5. Arrange the hens and the papaya halves on a serving platter and bring to the table.

TO COOK INDOORS: Prepare the hens and basting sauce as above. Arrange the butterflied hens on a foil-lined cookie sheet and bake for 25 minutes in a 350-degree oven. After the hens have been in the oven for 10 minutes, add the rum/sugar-brushed papaya halves and let cook the remaining 15 minutes. The hens are done when the juices run clear if the thigh is pricked with a fork. Serve as directed.

Turkey and Duck

Turkeys are indigenous to North America. And when Balboa first tasted an Aztec grilled turkey with hot chilies, he must have reacted with the same wild surprise as when he first stumbled upon the Pacific ocean. Turkey is so much a part of American cuisine, it is hard to imagine a feast day—Christmas or Thanksgiving—without it.

Wild duck is indigenous to America, too, but domesticated Long Island duck was born in China, and it was only with difficulty that the Chinese were persuaded to share their culinary favorite with us. We prefer Long Island duck in the following recipes, but if you can't find Long Island duck locally, replace with duck from your local market.

According to one 19th-century writer's account of the Chinese reluctance: "A gentleman . . . wrote from Sydney to China requesting that some of these birds [Peking ducks] be sent to him. The reply was that from the present disturbed state of China, it would be easier to send him a pair of Mandarins than a pair of Mandarin ducks." Nevertheless, by 1873, nine beautiful white Peking ducks arrived in America. The Long Island ducks sold today are supposedly descended from these original nine.

Duck with Hungarian Red Pepper Sauce

SERVES 6

This recipe uses indirect heat to grill duck quarters, which are arranged on the oiled grid on top of lemon slices so they do not stick.

2   Long Island ducks, about 4½ pounds each, all visible fat removed
     Marinade for Fatty Birds (see page 21)
3   lemons
     Hungarian Red Pepper Sauce (recipe follows)

1. Wash and dry the ducks. Reserve the giblets. Cut each duck into 4 quarters and divide the pieces between 2 large ziplock plastic bags. Divide the marinade between the 2 bags. Seal and turn the bags several times to coat the ducks. Place each bag on a cookie sheet at room temperature to marinate 1 hour (or 2 hours in refrigerator), turning occasionally.

2. Remove the zest from 1 lemon with a vegetable peeler and reserve the zest. Cut the lemon into 6 slices. Then cut the remaining 2 lemons into 6 slices each.

3. Prepare the grill for the Indirect Grilling Method (see page 17). Light the coals. When the briquets become ashen, add the lemon peel to the dripping pan water.

4. Remove the duck from the marinade, reserving the marinade. Arrange each duck quarter on top of 2 slices of lemon set on an oiled grid (you'll have 2 extra slices). Cover, then check to be sure dampers are open in the cover and in the bottom of the grill. Grill over indirect heat for 90 to 105 minutes, checking every 30 to 45 minutes to see if the water has evaporated or if more coals are needed. Brush the duck with marinade each time you open the grill. Duck is done when juices run clear after a fork is inserted into the thigh.

5. Heat the Hungarian Red Pepper Sauce in a small saucepan over medium heat. Transfer to a sauceboat. Arrange the cooked duck quarters on a serving platter. Bring to the table with the sauce. Serve immediately.

TO COOK INDOORS: Arrange the marinated duck on an oiled rack set in a roasting pan. Add about ½ inch of water to the bottom of the pan. Roast the duck at 425 degrees for 1 hour, then lower the heat to 325 degrees and continue cooking for an additional 45 minutes—a total of 1 hour and 45 minutes. Serve as directed.

Hungarian Red Pepper Sauce

MAKES 1¼ CUPS

3	tablespoons vegetable oil
2	cloves garlic, minced
1	large onion, thinly sliced
3	red bell peppers, seeded and cut into thin strips
1	tablespoon Hungarian sweet paprika
1	cup beef broth
¼	cup dry red wine
½	teaspoon dried marjoram
¼	teaspoon salt
¼	teaspoon freshly ground black pepper
3	tablespoons tomato paste

1. Heat the oil in a medium-sized frying pan. Add the garlic, onion and red pepper strips and cook for about 6 minutes or until tender. Sprinkle with the paprika. Add the broth, wine, marjoram, salt and pepper and bring to a boil. Blend in the tomato paste, reduce the heat and simmer for 3 to 4 minutes, stirring occasionally. Let the sauce sit in the saucepan until ready to use, then reheat. If the sauce is made in advance, refrigerate it in the saucepan.

▄▄▄

Turkey with Cinnamon-Raisin Bread Stuffing

SERVES 6 TO 8

CINNAMON-RAISIN BREAD STUFFING

5   tablespoons unsalted, butter
1   large onion, coarsely chopped
1   6-ounce package dried apple slices
3   cups day-old cinnamon-raisin bread, cut into 1/2-cubes
1/2 teaspoon dried sage

1   turkey, about 12–14 pounds, with giblets
3   tablespoons unsalted butter for rubbing turkey skin
1/4 teaspoon garlic powder
1/4 teaspoon freshly ground pepper

4   cinnamon sticks for aromatic

1. Prepare the stuffing: Heat the 5 tablespoons butter in a large sauce-pan or frying pan over medium heat. Add the onion and fry lightly until tender, about 6 minutes, stirring occasionally. Stir in the apple slices, bread cubes and sage, mixing well until all the ingredients are combined. Remove from the heat and reserve.

2. Wash and dry the turkey. Place it on the counter with the cavity facing you. Reserve the giblets for another use and remove all visible fat. Take off any rings or bracelets. You will be loosening the skin from the breast meat on both sides of the breastbone and you don't want to tear it.

3. Carefully, without tearing the skin, open a pocket on 1 side of the breastbone with your fingers. Work deeper and deeper, enlarging the pocket until your whole hand is inside under the skin. Although the skin is fastened both at the breastbone and at the bottom of the drumstick, you will be able to make pockets that are large, extending past the thigh and down slightly past the top of the drumstick.

4. Divide the stuffing in half and use the full quantity of stuffing to fill

both pockets, pushing it deeply into each side, all the way down to the drumsticks. Rub the turkey skin completely on all sides with the 3 tablespoons butter, then sprinkle the garlic powder and pepper over the skin.

5. Prepare the grill for the Indirect Grilling Method (see page 17). Light the coals. When the briquets become ashen, add the cinnamon sticks to the dripping pan water.

6. Place the turkey on an oiled grid, breast side up. Grill, covered, over indirect heat for 2 to 2½ hours without turning. Check every 30 to 45 minutes to see whether the water has evaporated or if more coals are needed. To check the turkey for doneness, insert a fork deeply into the thigh and twist slightly. If the juices run clear, the turkey is done. If the juices are pink, the turkey needs additional cooking.

7. Transfer to a large serving platter and let rest for 15 to 30 minutes before carving.

TO COOK INDOORS: Prepare the turkey as above and place on an oiled rack in a roasting pan. Add ½ inch water to the pan, along with 1 sliced onion. Cover the turkey loosely with foil and roast for 1 hour. Remove the foil and continue roasting for another 3 hours, about 4 hours in all or 20 minutes per pound. Baste at least 3 times with the pan juices during roasting. Let the turkey rest as above before carving.

Duck Quarters with Quince Brushing Sauce and Baby Vegetables

SERVES 6

These duck pieces are turned every 10 minutes, even though they're cooked over indirect heat. This gets rid of much of the fat under the skin.

6   wooden skewers, soaked in water for 30 minutes before use
2   Long Island ducks, 4½–5 pounds each, cut into quarters
1   recipe Marinade for Fatty Birds (see page 21)

QUINCE BRUSHING SAUCE

1	cup quince jelly
1	tablespoon water
¾	cup bottled chili sauce
¼	cup Japanese soy sauce
½	teaspoon grated fresh ginger root
1	clove garlic, minced
12	patty-pan squash
12	baby zucchini
12	baby yellow squash
2	tablespoons olive oil
¼	teaspoon dried basil leaves, crumbled

1. Wash and dry the duck pieces, removing any excess fat. Place 4 duck pieces in 1 large ziplock plastic bag and 4 in another. Divide the marinade between the bags. Seal each bag and turn several times to coat the pieces. Place each bag on a cookie sheet to marinate at room temperature for 1 hour (or 2 hours in the refrigerator), turning occasionally.

2. Prepare the grill for the Indirect Grilling Method (see page 17). Light the coals. While the coals heat, prepare Quince Brushing Sauce: Combine the jelly and water in a small saucepan over medium heat. Heat, stirring continuously, until the mixture is liquid. Stir in the chili and soy sauces, ginger and garlic. Continue cooking for 1 minute, then remove from the heat and reserve.

3. Wash the vegetables. Drain the skewers. Thread 2 each of the patty-pan squash, baby zucchini and baby yellow squash alternately on each skewer. Brush the skewers with the olive oil and sprinkle with the basil. Set aside.

4. Remove the duck from the marinade and pat dry. Brush each duck piece liberally with Quince Brushing Sauce and prick each in several places with a fork. When the coals are ashen, arrange the duck pieces, skin side up, on an ungreased grid over the drip pan. Place a small pan of water near grill for flare-ups.

5. Grill, covered, over indirect heat for about 50 minutes, turning every 10 minutes with long-handled tongs and brushing each time with

quince sauce. Check the coals after 30 minutes to see if they need to be replenished.

6. When duck pieces have grilled for 40 minutes, arrange the skewers directly over the coals on each side of the duck. Grill over direct heat for 6 minutes, turning the skewers every 2 minutes. Spoon any additional Quince Brushing Sauce into a small bowl. Arrange the skewers on a serving platter along with the duck quarters. Bring to the table with the bowl of Quince Brushing Sauce.

TO COOK INDOORS: Arrange the vegetables on skewers while the duck marinates, using oil and basil as directed. Place the skewers on a foil-covered cookie sheet and reserve.

Remove the duck pieces from the marinade, prick each well with a fork and arrange on a rack in a roasting pan with high sides. Fill the pan with ¼ inch water. Cook in a 450-degree oven for 15 minutes. Reduce the heat to 350 degrees and continue cooking for 90 minutes or until the juices run clear when the meat is pricked with a fork. Transfer the duck pieces to a serving platter and turn on the broiler. Broil the vegetables on a cookie sheet for about 6 minutes, turning once after 3 minutes. When the vegetables are lightly charred, remove from the heat and bring to the table with the duck pieces and Quince Brushing Sauce.

Duck Quarters with Kumquat-Brandy Basting Sauce

SERVES 6

2   Long Island ducks, 4½–5 pounds each, cut into quarters
1   recipe Marinade for Fatty Birds (see page 21)

KUMQUAT-BRANDY BASTING SAUCE
1   10-ounce jar kumquats with syrup
¼   cup brandy

1. Wash and dry the duck pieces, removing all visible fat. Place 4 pieces in 1 large ziplock plastic bag and 4 in another. Divide the marinade between the bags. Seal and turn each bag several times to coat the

duck. Place the bags on a cookie sheet to marinate for 1 hour at room temperature (or 2 hours in the refrigerator), turning occasionally.

2. Prepare the grill for the Indirect Grilling Method (see page 17). Light the coals. Prepare the Kumquat-Brandy Basting Sauce: Place the kumquats and their syrup in a food processor fitted with the steel blade and add the brandy. Pulse several times until the kumquats are finely minced.

3. Remove the duck quarters from the marinade and pat dry. Prick each piece in several places with a fork. Brush each liberally with the Kumquat-Brandy Basting Sauce. When the coals are ashen, arrange the duck quarters, skin side up, on an ungreased grid over the dripping pan. Bring a small bowl of water to the grill to prevent flare-ups.

4. Grill, covered, over indirect heat for about 50 minutes, turning the duck pieces every 10 minutes and brushing each time with the basting sauce. Check to see if the water or coals need to be replenished after 30 minutes.

5. Transfer any remaining basting sauce to a small bowl. Arrange the duck pieces on a serving platter. Bring to the table with the sauce.

TO COOK INDOORS: Remove the duck pieces from the marinade, prick each well with a fork and arrange on a rack in a roasting pan with high sides. Fill the pan with 1/4 inch water. Cook in a 450-degree oven for 15 minutes. Reduce the heat to 350 degrees and continue cooking for 90 minutes or until the juices run clear when the meat is pricked with a fork. Transfer to a serving platter as directed.

Duck Quarters with Two-Peppercorn Sauce

SERVES 6

2   Long Island ducks, 4½–5 pounds each, cut into quarters
1   recipe Marinade for Fatty Birds (see page 21)
1   recipe Two-Peppercorn Sauce (recipe follows)

1. Wash and dry the duck quarters and remove all visible fat. Put 4 pieces in 1 large ziplock plastic bag and 4 in another. Divide the marinade between the bags. Seal and turn each bag several times to coat duck. Place the bags on a cookie sheet to marinate at room temperature for 1 hour (or 2 hours in the refrigerator), turning occasionally.

2. Prepare the grill for the Indirect Grilling Method (see page 17). Remove the duck pieces from the marinade and prick each in several places with a fork. When the coals are ashen, place the duck pieces, skin side up, on an ungreased grid over the dripping pan. Place a small bowl of water near the grill in case of flare-ups.

3. Grill, covered, over indirect heat for 50 minutes, turning the duck pieces with long-handled tongs every 10 minutes. Check the coals and water after 30 minutes to see if they need to be replenished. Arrange the cooked duck pieces on a serving platter and bring to the table with Two-Peppercorn Sauce.

TO COOK INDOORS: Remove the duck pieces from the marinade, prick each well with a fork and arrange on a rack in a roasting pan with high sides. Fill the pan with ¼ inch water. Place in a 450-degree oven for 15 minutes. Reduce the heat to 350 degrees and continue cooking for 90 minutes or until juices run clear when the meat is pricked with a fork. Transfer to a serving platter as directed.

Two-Peppercorn Sauce

Crème fraîche is commercially available, or you can make your own with buttermilk and whipping cream.

MAKES 1½ CUPS

1   tablespoon black peppercorns
1   tablespoon green peppercorns
1½ cups crème fraîche

1. Place the peppercorns in a large ziplock plastic bag and seal. Crush them with a kitchen mallet. Place the crème fraîche in a serving bowl and stir in the crushed peppercorns. Cover and chill until serving time.

Easy-Grilled Turkey Thighs with Picante Sauce

SERVES 6

6   turkey thighs, about 1 pound each
¾   cup bottled picante sauce
2   tablespoons virgin olive oil
1   teaspoon garlic powder

1. Prepare the grill for the Indirect Grilling Method (see page 17). Light the coals. Wash and dry the turkey thighs. Carefully insert your fingers between the skin and the flesh of the turkey thighs to make a pocket. Spoon 2 tablespoons of picante sauce into each pocket. Smooth the skin back into place. Brush the thighs with olive oil and sprinkle lightly with the garlic powder.

2. When the coals are ashen, arrange the thighs on an ungreased grid, stuffing side up, and cook, covered, over indirect heat for 1 hour. Check to see if the water or coals need replenishing after 30 minutes. The thighs are done if the juices run clear when the meat is pricked with a fork.

3. Arrange the turkey thighs on a serving platter and bring to the table.

TO COOK INDOORS: Fill the turkey thighs with the picante sauce and sprinkle with garlic powder as directed. Arrange the thighs, stuffing side up, on a foil-lined cookie sheet and bake for 70 minutes at 375 degrees. The thighs are done if the juices run clear when the meat is pricked with a fork.

Grilled Whole Duck with Fennel

SERVES 4

1   Long Island duck, about 4 pounds
¼   teaspoon freshly ground pepper
1   tangerine, peeled and divided into sections
1   tablespoon virgin olive oil

½   cup fennel seeds for aromatic (optional)

1   large bulb of fresh fennel, sliced (optional)
2   tablespoons virgin olive oil
2   tablespoons freshly grated Parmesan cheese

1. Prepare the grill for the Indirect Grilling Method (see page 17). Light the coals. Wash and dry the duck, removing all visible fat.

2. With a sharp knife make 2 3-inch slits on both sides of the duck where the wing meets the breast at the breastbone. Bend the wing tips under the bird. Sprinkle the pepper inside the duck cavity. Place the tangerine sections inside the cavity. Brush the bottom of the duck lightly with 1 tablespoon olive oil. Use a fork to prick the duck on the entire body surface.

3. When the coals are ashen, place the duck on the grid, breast side up, over the dripping pan. Cover the grill, leaving the dampers open in both the cover and the grill bottom. Grill, covered, over indirect heat for 3 hours, checking every 30 to 45 minutes to see if additional water or coals are needed.

4. After the duck has cooked for 15 minutes, sprinkle the ½ cup fennel seeds onto the coals if desired.

5. Test the duck for doneness by inserting a fork into the thigh. If the juices run clear, the duck is done. If the juices are pink, the duck needs more time on the grill.

6. Remove the duck from the grill and place it on a cutting board. Let stand 20 to 30 minutes before carving.

7. While the duck rests, grill the fennel: Brush both sides of the fennel slices with the 2 tablespoons olive oil. Place the slices on the grid directly over 1 bank of coals and grill over direct heat for 3 minutes. Turn, sprinkle the cooked side with Parmesan cheese and continue grilling for 3 minutes longer or until brown. Remove from the grill.

8. Use poultry shears to cut the duck into quarters. Arrange it on a serving platter and garnish with the grilled fennel slices.

TO COOK INDOORS: Prepare the duck as described above. Place on a rack in a high-sided roasting pan over ¼ inch water. Put in a preheated 450-degree oven for 15 minutes, then reduce the temperature to 350 degrees for an additional 90 minutes. The duck is done when it is golden and the joints move freely. To test, insert a fork into the thigh. If the juices run clear, the duck is cooked. If they run pink, it needs more cooking time.

While the cooked duck is resting, brush fennel slices with olive oil, place under broiler and cook for 3 minutes. Turn, cook an additional 3 minutes, sprinkle with Parmesan cheese and continue to broil until brown (about 1 minute).

Farm-Raised Game

People are only now beginning to realize that game has its own flavor, as do domestic chicken, turkey and duck. The game birds in this book, for example, have been farm-raised as opposed to caught in the wild. And when farm-raised birds are made ready for the table, they are not aged as wild game is—a process which distorts the taste— so their own delicious taste can come through and be appreciated.

People eating farm-raised game for the first time should pay attention to the delicate flavors and nuances of each particular bird.

Grilled Mallard with Green Salsa

SERVES 6

3   mallards, 2½ pounds each, halved

MARINADE

1   cup dry white wine

½   cup virgin olive oil

⅓   cup white wine vinegar

1   scallion, minced

1   clove garlic, minced

½   teaspoon red pepper flakes

6   wooden skewers, soaked in water for 30 minutes before use

GREEN SALSA

2   4-ounce cans mild green chili peppers, coarsely chopped

3   scallions

3   cloves garlic

3   fresh jalapeño peppers

½   cup fresh cilantro

3   tablespoons virgin olive oil

18   large cloves garlic, unpeeled
     Vegetable oil for brushing garlic

Examine all game closely for pinfeathers. If you find any, use tweezers or needlenose pliers to pull them out.

1. Check the mallards for pinfeathers, removing them with tweezers or needlenose pliers. Wash and dry the ducks. Place them in 2 large ziplock plastic bags, 3 halves in each.

2. Prepare the marinade: Combine the wine, olive oil, vinegar, scallions, garlic and red pepper flakes in a small bowl. Divide the marinade between the 2 bags. Seal the bags and turn them a few times to coat the duck. Place them on a cookie sheet, arranging the halves so they lie flat. Marinate in the refrigerator for 2 to 24 hours, turning ocassionally.

3. Prepare the Green Salsa: Drain the canned chilies and place them in a food processor fitted with the steel blade. Cut the scallions into 1-inch pieces; peel and halve the garlic cloves. Add both to the food

processor. Split the jalapeños lengthwise, remove seeds under cold running water, cut in half and add to the food processor. (Wash your hands several times after cutting the jalapeños and do not touch your eyes. If possible, wear rubber gloves.) Pulse the ingredients in the food processor a few times until coarsely chopped. Do not puree.

4. Prepare the grill for the Direct Grilling Method (see page 16). Light the coals. When the briquets become ashen, remove the mallards from the marinade, reserving the marinade. Place the ducks on an oiled grid, skin side up, over the ashen coals. Grill, uncovered, over direct heat for 24 minutes, turning every 6 minutes and brushing with marinade each time. *NOTE: If the mallards weigh slightly more than 2¹/₂ pounds each, they will need a few additional minutes on the grill. Don't forget to turn them every 6 minutes and brush with marinade each time.* The duck will be done if the juices run clear when the meat is pricked with a fork.

5. Drain the skewers. Push 3 whole, unpeeled garlic cloves onto each skewer. Brush the cloves liberally with the vegetable oil and place the skewers on the outer edge of the grill. Turn the garlic every 2 minutes. The garlic will take anywhere from 20 to 30 minutes to be soft enough to squeeze out of its skin. Check it by pressing gently.

6. Transfer the ducks to 2 serving platters along with the garlic skewers. Serve each guest a duck half and a garlic skewer. The guests can squeeze the garlic onto their own duck and spread it over the top. Pass the Green Salsa.

TO COOK INDOORS: Arrange the mallards, skin side up, on a foil-lined cookie sheet. Bake for 1 hour at 350 degrees, brushing with the marinade every 20 minutes. After the mallards have cooked 40 minutes, add the loose garlic cloves around the edges of the cookie sheet. Turn the garlic after 10 minutes. Serve with mallard as above.

Pheasant with Grilled Chestnuts and Chestnut Sauce

SERVES 6

3   pheasants, 2½–2¾ pounds each, halved
1   recipe Marinade for Lean Birds (see page 21)

CHESTNUT SAUCE
1   8-ounce can chestnuts (do not buy chestnuts in syrup)
4   tablespoons unsalted butter
2   tablespoons all-purpose flour
1   cup half-and-half or milk
½   cup heavy cream
¼   teaspoon salt
¼   teaspoon freshly ground pepper
¼   teaspoon ground cinnamon
½   teaspoon freshly grated nutmeg
30   whole fresh chestnuts

1. Wash and dry the pheasant halves. Place 3 halves in each of 2 large ziplock plastic bags and divide the marinade between them. Seal the bags and turn several times to coat the pheasant. Place the bags on cookie sheets, arranging the halves so they lie flat. Marinate for 1 hour at room temperature (or 2 hours in the refrigerator), turning occasionally.

2. Prepare the Chestnut Sauce: Puree the canned chestnuts in a food processor fitted with the steel blade. Set aside. Heat the butter in a saucepan. When melted, whisk in the flour with a wire whisk until well mixed. Whisk in the half-and-half, stirring over medium heat until the sauce thickens. Add the heavy cream, chestnut puree, salt, pepper, cinnamon and nutmeg. Let sit in the saucepan until ready to reheat at serving time.

3. With a small, very sharp knife, cut a cross in the flat side of each chestnut, cutting through the skin. Tear off 6 sheets of aluminum foil, each large enough to wrap around 5 chestnuts. Place 5 chest-

nuts in the center of each foil sheet. Bring the corners of the foil to the center and twist shut.

4. Prepare the grill for the Direct Grilling Method (see page 16). Light the coals. When the briquets become ashen, remove the pheasants from the marinade, reserving the marinade. Place the halves on an oiled grid over the ashen coals and grill, uncovered, over direct heat for 24 minutes, turning every 6 minutes and brushing with marinade each time.

5. Put the chestnut packets on the outer edges of the grill 30 minutes after the pheasants are put on. Grill for 15 to 20 minutes, turning the packets twice. When the pheasants are done, transfer to a serving platter with the chestnut packets. Bring to the table with the reheated chestnut sauce. Each guest gets a chestnut packet and can open and use his fingers to peel off the softened chestnut shells.

TO COOK INDOORS: Arrange the marinated pheasant halves on a foil-lined cookie sheet and bake at 350 degrees for 45 to 50 minutes, brushing with marinade every 15 minutes. Place chestnut packets in oven for the last 30 minutes.

Grilled Mallards on a Bed of Warm Sauerkraut

SERVES 6

This recipe calls for juniper berries—small blue berries with a distinctive flavor—often used in Europe, either fresh or dried, for game stuffings and marinades. The berries, which give gin its special flavor, come from a European evergreen. Incidentally, if you can find dried juniper stalks, use them as an aromatic to throw on ashen coals when cooking game. If you can't find juniper berries at specialty food stores in your area, see page 182 for our mail-order sources.

3   mallards, about 2½ pounds each, halved
1   recipe Marinade for Lean Birds (see page 21)
1   tablespoon garlic powder
1   tablespoon sweet paprika

1   tablespoon freshly ground black pepper
12   strips bacon
4   tablespoons unsalted butter
6   cups good-quality sauerkraut (bottled if desired)
12   dried juniper berries, crushed
4   teaspoons caraway seeds

1. Wash and dry the mallards. Place 3 halves in 1 large ziplock plastic bag and 3 in another. Combine the marinade with the garlic powder, sweet paprika and black pepper. Divide the marinade between the 2 plastic bags. Seal the bags and turn a few times to coat the ducks. Place the bags on a cookie sheet, arranging the duck halves so they lie in a single layer. Marinate for 1 hour at room temperature (or 2 hours in the refrigerator), turning occasionally.

2. Meanwhile, fry the bacon in large, heavy skillet until done. Drain on paper towels and pat with paper towels to remove excess grease. Cut the bacon into 1-inch cubes and return it to the skillet. Add the butter, sauerkraut, juniper berries and caraway seeds. Simmer, uncovered, for 12 to 15 minutes or until all visible liquid has evaporated. Sauerkraut should be very dry.

3. Prepare the grill for the Direct Grilling Method (see page 16). Light the coals. When the briquets become ashen, remove the mallards from the marinade, reserving the marinade. Place them on an oiled grid over the ashen coals and cook, uncovered, over direct heat for 20 to 24 minutes, turning every 5 minutes and brushing with marinade each time.

4. When the mallards are done, transfer the sauerkraut mixture to a serving platter. Arrange the mallards attractively on top of the sauerkraut. Serve immediately with cold beer.

TO COOK INDOORS: Arrange the mallards, skin side up, on a foil-lined cookie sheet and bake for 1 hour at 350 degrees, brushing with marinade every 20 minutes. Serve as directed.

Grilled Pheasant with Peach Cumberland Sauce

SERVES 6

3   pheasants, about 2¼ pounds each, halved

MARINADE

2   cups virgin olive oil
3   tablespoons red wine vinegar
4   cloves garlic, minced
2   teaspoons dried thyme
2   teaspoons dried rosemary
½   cup grated orange zest

PEACH CUMBERLAND SAUCE

1   cup red currant jelly
1   cup fresh orange juice
3   tablespoons fresh lemon juice
3   medium-sized shallots, minced
2   teaspoons Dijon mustard
½   teaspoon grated fresh gingerroot
½   cup port wine
     Grated zest of ½ navel orange

3   fresh peaches
6   teaspoons brown sugar

1. Wash and dry the pheasants. Prepare the marinade: Combine the oil, vinegar, garlic, thyme, rosemary and ½ cup grated orange zest in a jar and shake together. Put 3 pheasant halves in each of 2 large ziplock plastic bags and divide the marinade between them. Seal the bags and turn them several times to coat the pheasants. Arrange the bags on cookie sheets and marinate at room temperature for 1 hour (or 2 hours in the refrigerator), turning occasionally.

2. Prepare the Peach Cumberland Sauce: Combine the currant jelly, orange juice, lemon juice and shallots in a saucepan. Bring to a boil over medium heat, reduce the heat and simmer for 10 minutes or until the volume is reduced by half. Strain and return to the saucepan.

3. Stir in the mustard, ginger and port. Bring to a boil again. Reduce the heat, stir in the grated navel orange zest and remove the saucepan from the heat. Transfer the sauce to a serving bowl—it should be served at room temperature and can safely sit out of the refrigerator because of its high sugar content.

4. Bring a saucepan of water to the boil and drop the peaches into the boiling water. Turn off the heat and let sit for 30 seconds to a few minutes or until the skin begins to wrinkle and the peaches can be peeled. Quickly run the peaches under cold tap water until they cool. Peel them, cut them in half, remove the stones and reserve.

5. Prepare the grill for the Direct Grilling Method (see page 16). Light the coals. When the briquets become ashen, remove the pheasant from the marinade, reserving the marinade. Arrange the pheasant halves, skin side up, on an oiled grid over the ashen coals. Grill, covered, over direct heat for 25 to 30 minutes, turning every 4 or 5 minutes and brushing with marinade each time.

6. The last time the pheasants are turned, place the peach halves, cut side up, on the grid and grill for 2 minutes. Turn the peaches with a spatula and grill for another 2 minutes.

7. Transfer the pheasants to a serving platter. Arrange the peaches around the pheasant halves and sprinkle each peach with 1 teaspoon brown sugar. Serve immediately with the Peach Cumberland Sauce.

TO COOK INDOORS: Arrange the pheasant halves, skin side up, on a foil-lined cookie sheet and bake for 45 to 50 minutes at 350 degrees. Brush the pheasants with the reserved marinade after the first 30 minutes, but do not turn. When the pheasant is cooked, transfer it to a serving platter and cover with foil to keep warm. Quickly brown the peach halves under the broiler, then arrange them on the platter surrounding the pheasant. Sprinkle each half with 1 teaspoon brown sugar and serve with Peach Cumberland Sauce.

Partridge in Crème Fraîche with Oranges and Pomegranates

SERVES 6

In this recipe, the noodles are made ahead of time, then placed in a colander in the sink to wait until the partridges finish cooking. At serving time, a pot of boiling water is poured over the noodles to reheat them.

1   large pomegranate

1½ cups crème fraîche

6   partridges, about 1 pound each

3   oranges, peeled and quartered

⅓   cup grated orange zest, soaked briefly in water for use as aromatic

4   cups cooked wide egg noodles, placed in a colander to drain

2   tablespoons unsalted butter

1. Cut the pomegranate in half. Use a manual or electric juicer to extract the juice. Strain and reserve 6 tablespoons of the seeds for garnish. Combine the juice with the crème fraîche.

2. Arrange the partridges in a glass dish and brush them completely with the crème fraîche mixture. Cover with plastic wrap and marinate at room temperature for 1 hour (or 2 hours in the refrigerator), turning occasionally.

3. Place a rectangular metal pan, wide enough to catch the fat that drops from the partridge, on the bottom of the grill at the center. Arrange 25 coals on either side of the pan (about 50 coals in all). Light the charcoal. When the briquets are almost ashen, fill the dripping pan with ¼ inch of water.

4. Prepare the grill for the Indirect Grilling Method (see page 17). Light the coals. When the coals become ashen, place 2 orange quarters in the cavity of each partridge. Sprinkled the drained orange zest on each bank of coals. Immediately place the partridges on an oiled grid over the dripping pan. Grill, covered, over indirect heat for 35 to 40 minutes, testing for doneness after 25 minutes. The juices should run clear when the meat is pricked with a fork.

5. While the pheasant cooks, fill a saucepan with water and bring to a boil. When ready to serve, pour the boiled water over the noodles, shake the colander to remove excess water and transfer the noodles to a serving platter with raised sides. Toss with the butter.

6. Arrange the partridges attractively over the hot noodles. Sprinkle all over with pomegranate seeds for garnish.

TO COOK INDOORS: Place the crème fraîche–topped partridges on a foil-lined cookie sheet and roast in a 375-degree oven for 20 minutes or until done. Serve as above.

Grilled Poussin in Applejack and Cream

SERVES 6

Applejack is an apple bandy distilled from cider. It is widely drunk in France—especially in Normandy, where apples are grown—but it is known there as Calvados.

This recipe calls for splitting each poussin down the backbone, then opening it up, butterfly fashion. Birds that are prepared in this very old French way are said to be *à la crapaudine*—done in the style of a *crapaud* or toad, which they resemble. *Larousse Gastronomique* suggests using this method for squab, which is then grilled and served with sauce diable.

6   poussins, about 1 pound each
6   tablespoons unsalted butter
½   teaspoon dried ground sage for sprinkling on poussins
¼   cup dried sage for aromatic
     Peel from 1 large apple for aromatic
2   cups heavy cream
¼   cup applejack

1. Wash and dry each poussin. Split the poussins down the backbone

with poultry shears (or have your butcher do it). Open each pous-sin, butterfly fashion, and use the heel of your hand or a wooden mallet to break the breastbone so that the poussins lie open and flat.

Butterflied poussin and other birds are especially attractive when a slit is made halfway between the breastbone and legs on each side so that legs can be tucked into the slits, making a neat package (see illustration).

2. Rub the skin of each poussin generously with butter and sprinkle the ½ teaspoon sage over them.

3. Prepare the grill for the Direct Grilling Method (see page 16). Light the coals. Sprinkle a few drops of water onto the ¼ cup dried sage so it is moist. When the briquets become ashen, sprinkle the sage and apple peel over them. Immediately arrange the butterflied poussins on an oiled grid, skin side up, over the ashen coals. Grill, covered, over direct heat for 12 to 15 minutes, turning the poussins every 3 minutes or until done to taste.

4. While the poussins cook, combine the cream and nutmeg in a me-dium-sized saucepan and heat over low heat, taking care not to let the cream boil or it will curdle. Stir in the applejack and transfer the sauce to a sauceboat. Arrange the grilled poussins on a large serving platter. Spoon the warm applejack and cream over each poussin. Serve immediately, passing the remaining sauce in a sauceboat.

TO COOK INDOORS: Prepare as directed and place the poussins in butterfly fashion on a foil-covered cookie sheet. Roast in a 375-degree oven for about 20 minutes or until golden brown. Serve as directed.

Grilled Squab with Pepita Spread and Stuffed Baby Pumpkins

SERVES 6

The delectable meat of the pumpkin seed is called the pepita. It is avail-able in the packaged nuts department of most supermarkets.

6   **squabs, 1 pound each**
1   **recipe Marinade for Lean Birds (see page 21)**
1   **recipe Stuffed Baby Pumpkins (recipe follows)**

PEPITA SPREAD

1   **cup pepitas, roasted**
1   **clove garlic, peeled**
2   **teaspoons corn oil**

1. Wash and dry the squabs. Place 3 squabs in each of 2 large ziplock plastic bags. Divide the marinade between the bags. Seal the bags and turn several times to coat the squabs. Place the bags on a cookie sheet and marinate for 1 hour at room temperature (or 2 hours in the refrigerator), turning occasionally.

2. Prepare the grill for the Indirect Grilling Method (see page 17). Light the coals. Steam and fill the pumpkins according to the following recipe. Arrange them on a serving platter and reserve.

3. Prepare the Pepita Spread: Place the pepitas and garlic in a food processor fitted with the steel blade and process until pureed. With the motor still running, add the oil and process until smooth and well combined.

4. Remove the squabs from the marinade, reserving the marinade. Carefully insert your fingers between the skin and the flesh of each squab, making deep pockets on each side of the breastbone. Take care not to tear the skin. Spread 1½ teaspoons of Pepita Spread under the skin on each side, using 1 tablespoon per squab. Thread the squabs on a rotisserie spit, truss each with strong twine, then use the clamps to secure each in place.

5. When the coals become ashen, turn the rotisserie on and grill the squabs over indirect heat for 35 to 40 minutes. To test for doneness, insert a fork into the thighs; if the juices run clear, the squabs are done. Remove the squabs from the spit and arrange on a serving platter. Bring to the table with the Stuffed Baby Pumpkins.

TO COOK INDOORS: Arrange the marinated squabs, breast side up, on a foil-covered cookie sheet. Roast in a 375-degree oven for 25 to 30 minutes or until the squabs test done. Brush with marinade after the first 15 minutes.

Stuffed Baby Pumpkins

SERVES 6

6   baby pumpkins, about 8–10 ounces each, rinsed and dried
3   tablespoons unsalted butter
1   medium onion, minced
¼   teaspoon garlic powder
¼   teaspoon salt
¼   teaspoon freshly ground pepper
3   slices day-old bread, cut into ½-inch cubes
½   cup pepitas, roasted

1. Place the pumpkins in a steamer inside a large pot filled with 1 inch water. The water should not come above the steamer or touch the pumpkins. Cover the pot, bring the water to a boil and steam the pumpkins for 12 to 15 minutes or until fork-tender. Remove the pumpkins and cool.

2. While the pumpkins steam, heat the butter in a heavy frying pan. Add the onion and sauté for 6 minutes or until tender, stirring occasionally. Sprinkle the garlic powder, salt and pepper over the onion. Add the bread cubes and toss, stirring, until they are coated with butter. Stir in the pepitas.

3. When the pumpkins are cool enough to handle, cut a 1½-inch circle on top of each pumpkin around the stem and lift off. This will act as a "lid." Remove and discard the seeds and any other material inside the pumpkin as well as on the underside of the lid.

4. Divide the stuffing into 6 equal parts and use 1 part to stuff each pumpkin, mounding it loosely into the pumpkins. Arrange the lids so that each is leaning against a pumpkin on the side. Serve with grilled squab.

Quail with Grilled Pineapple Slices and Pineapple Sauce

SERVES 6

12 quail

1 whole pineapple, peeled, eyes removed (see *Note* for optional preparation)

½ cup unsalted butter, melted

2 teaspoons grated lemon zest

1 teaspoon dried tarragon

¼ teaspoon salt

¼ teaspoon freshly ground pepper, or to taste

1 recipe Hot Pineapple Sauce (recipe follows)

3 cups cooked wild rice (optional)

1. Wash and dry the quail. Cut each lengthwise down the backbone, using kitchen scissors or poultry shears (or ask your butcher to do it). Open the quail to butterfly position, then press on the breastbone until the bone cracks and the quail lies flat.

2. Prepare the grill for the Direct Grilling Method (see page 16). Light the coals. Core the pineapple and cut it into ½-inch slices.

3. Combine the butter, lemon zest, tarragon, salt and pepper. Brush the quail with the butter mixture. When the coals become ashen, arrange the quail, skin side up, on an oiled grid over the ashen coals. Cook, uncovered, over direct heat, skin side up, for about 9 minutes, turning every 3 minutes.

4. While the quail grill, arrange the pineapple slices on the grid and grill for 2 minutes on each side. Heat the Hot Pineapple Sauce and transfer it to a serving bowl. Arrange the quail and the pineapple slices on a serving platter and bring to the table with the Hot Pineapple Sauce. Serve with wild rice, if desired.

TO COOK INDOORS: Arrange the butterflied quail, skin side up, on a foil-covered cookie sheet, along with the pineapple slices. Brush the quail with the butter mixture. Broil 6 inches from the heat source for 10 minutes, turning once after 5 minutes. Arrange the pineapple slices and quail on a serving platter and bring to the table with the Hot Pineapple Sauce.

Note: If you have a rotisserie attachment on your grill, try grilling the whole pineapple on a rotisserie instead of grilling pineapple slices. Peel the pineapple as directed above, but leave the leaves intact. Remove the eyes. Thread the pineapple on a rotisserie and baste with a mixture of 4 tablespoons unsalted butter and 1/2 teaspoon grated lemon zest. Grill for 15 minutes. Remove carefully and transfer to a serving platter. Cut into slices at the table and serve with the quail and Hot Pineapple Sauce.

Hot Pineapple Sauce

MAKES 2 1/2 CUPS

2   tablespoons cornstarch
1   20-ounce can crushed pineapple, drained with juice reserved
2   tablespoons soy sauce
1   tablespoon honey
2   teaspoons white wine vinegar
1/2   teaspoon grated lemon zest

1. Place the cornstarch in a small bowl and add a few spoonfuls of reserved pineapple juice. Mix until no lumps remain. Transfer to a saucepan. Slowly stir in remaining pineapple juice.

2. Stir in the soy sauce, pineapple, honey, vinegar and lemon zest, mixing well. Bring to a boil, stirring constantly. Reduce the heat and simmer for about 5 minutes, stirring occasionally. Remove the sauce from the heat and set aside in saucepan. When ready to use, reheat the sauce, adding a little warm water to thin it, and transfer it to a sauceboat.

Poussin, Middle Eastern Style, with Currant Stuffing

SERVES 6

CURRANT STUFFING
- ¼ cup unsalted butter or margarine
- 1 medium onion, minced
- ⅓ cup pine nuts
- 3 cups cooked rice
- ⅓ cup dried currants
- ½ teaspoon ground cinnamon

- 6 poussins, about 1 pound each
- ½ cup virgin olive oil
- 6 tablespoons fresh lemon juice
- ½ teaspoon freshly ground pepper
- ½ cup dried oregano, soaked 10 minutes in water and drained
- 1 tablespoon paprika
- 3 lemons, thinly sliced

1. Prepare the Currant Stuffing: Heat the butter in a heavy saucepan over medium heat. Add the onion and pine nuts and sauté until the onion is tender, about 6 minutes. Stir in the rice, currants and cinnamon. Continue cooking and stirring until the rice is combined. Reserve.

2. Wash and dry the poussins. Cut each poussin lengthwise down the backbone with poultry shears or kitchen scissors (or ask your butcher to do it). Spread each apart in the butterfly position on a flat surface. Strike each poussin sharply on the breastbone with the heel of your hand. You will hear a crack and the poussin will lie flat.

3. Place 1 poussin on the counter, skin side up, with the legs facing you. Carefully insert your fingers between the skin and the flesh on each side of the breastbone, making 2 small pockets. Repeat with remaining poussins, taking care not to tear the skin. Spoon 2 tablespoons of stuffing into each pocket, using 4 tablespoons per bird.

4. Combine the olive oil and lemon juice and brush each poussin with this mixture. Then sprinkle each with pepper and paprika.

5. Prepare the grill for the Direct Grilling Method (see page 16). Light the coals. When the briquets become ashen, sprinkle drained oregano on the coals and arrange the poussins, skin side up, on an oiled grid over the ashen coals. Grill, covered, over direct heat for 20 minutes, turning the poussins every 5 minutes with long-handled tongs. The meat is done when the juices run clear when pricked with a fork.

6. Transfer the poussins to a large serving platter and bring to the table. Serve immediately.

TO COOK INDOORS: Prepare the poussins as directed. Arrange each poussin on a foil-lined cookie sheet, skin side up, and bake for 20 minutes at 375 degrees. Test for doneness as above.

Butterflied Poussin with Sun-Dried Tomatoes

SERVES 6

6   poussins, 1 pound each
1/4   cup virgin olive oil
3/4   teaspoon dried oregano leaves
1/4   cup dried oregano leaves, soaked in water to cover for 10 minutes and drained for aromatic
12   sun-dried tomatoes, chopped (drain if packed in oil)
6   scallions, minced

1. Butterfly each poussin by cutting along the backbone with kitchen scissors or poultry shears (or ask your butcher to do it). Spread apart in butterfly position. Place each poussin on a flat surface and strike with the heel of your hand to flatten. You will hear the breastbone crack.

2. Prepare the grill for the Direct Grilling Method (see page 16). Light the coals. When the briquets become ashen, brush each poussin with olive oil and sprinkle the 3/4 teaspoon oregano over them. Sprinkle the drained oregano leaves over the ashen coals. Arrange

the poussins, skin side up, on an oiled grid over the coals. Grill, covered, over direct heat for 16 minutes, turning each poussin with long-handled tongs every 4 minutes. Poussins are done if the juices run clear when the meat is pricked with a fork.

3. While the poussins grill, put the chopped sun-dried tomatoes and minced scallions into 2 small bowls and bring to the table. Transfer the poussins to a large serving platter and bring to the table. Sprinkle the poussins with the tomatoes and scallions and serve immediately.

TO COOK INDOORS: Butterfly the poussins as directed and brush with oil. Place each poussin on a foil-lined cookie sheet and bake at 375 degrees for 20 minutes. Use a fork to test for doneness; if the juices run clear when the meat is pricked, the poussins are done.

Birds of a Different Feather

Grazing Grill

The hors d'oeuvre has undergone a metamorphosis in recent years. What was once a vaguely noticed cocktail party tidbit has turned into a whole style of eating— smaller portions of a variety of delicacies interesting enough to be the centerpiece of any meal. Eating this way has been called grazing. Grazing foods can make up an entire meal served as part of an elaborate barbecue buffet. But they are just as effective when served as the first grilled course in a delicious barbecued dinner.

▲▲▲

Buffalo Chicken Wings

SERVES 6

This recipe can be easily doubled.

24	chicken wings, about 2 pounds
⅓	cup vegetable oil
¾	teaspoon garlic powder
½	teaspoon cayenne pepper

BUTTER SAUCE

4	tablespoons unsalted butter
1½	tablespoons red wine vinegar
1	teaspoon Tabasco sauce

BLUE CHEESE DRESSING

1	cup mayonnaise
½	cup sour cream
1	small onion, minced
3	cloves garlic, minced
¼	cup packed minced fresh parsley
2	teaspoons fresh lemon juice
1	tablespoon red wine vinegar
⅓	cup crumbled blue cheese
¼	teaspoon salt
⅛	teaspoon freshly ground pepper
6	large stalks celery

1. Wash and dry the wings. Cut each wing into 2 pieces at the joint, creating a small drumstick and a wing. Brush the pieces with the oil and sprinkle them with the garlic powder and cayenne pepper. Arrange the pieces on a tray and reserve.

2. Prepare the Butter Sauce: Melt the butter in a small saucepan over medium heat. Stir in the wine vinegar and Tabasco sauce. Remove from the heat and reserve.

3. Prepare the Blue Cheese Dressing: In a medium-sized bowl, combine the mayonnaise, sour cream, onion, garlic, parsley, lemon juice, vinegar, blue cheese, salt and pepper. Mix well and reserve.

4. Peel the celery stalks to remove the strings, then cut each into 3-inch lengths. Arrange on a small serving plate.

5. Prepare the grill for the Direct Grilling Method (see page 16). Light the coals. When the briquets become ashen, arrange the wings on an oiled grid over the ashen coals. Grill, covered, over direct heat for 9 minutes, turning every 3 minutes.

6. Transfer the wings to a large serving bowl. Pour over the hot Butter Sauce and toss to coat. Bring to the table with the celery and Blue Cheese Dressing. Dip the wings and celery into the dressing.

TO COOK INDOORS: Arrange the wings on a foil-lined cookie sheet. Bake at 375 degrees for 40 minutes without turning. Serve hot as directed.

Five-Spice Chicken Wings

SERVES 6

This Oriental appetizer makes excellent grazing food and should be eaten with fingers. Light Japanese soy sauce and Chinese five-spice powder (made of approximately equal quantities of cinnamon, ground aniseed, star anise, cloves and Szechuan pepper are available at Chinese and other Oriental food shops. Or see page 182 for our list of mail-order sources. Five-spice powder is sometimes called five-fragrance powder, five heavenly spices and other similar names.

18 **chicken wings, about 1½ pounds**

MARINADE
½ **cup Japanese soy sauce**
2 **teaspoons honey**
1 **teaspoon Chinese five-spice powder**
½ **teaspoon ground ginger**
½ **teaspoon garlic powder**

1   teaspoon minced onion

1   tablespoon dry sherry

1. Wash and dry the wings and place them in a large ziplock plastic bag. Prepare the marinade: Combine all the marinade ingredients in a small bowl. Pour the marinade into the bag. Seal the bag and turn it a few times to coat the wings. Place the bag in a bowl and marinate at room temperature for 1 hour (or 2 hours in the refrigerator), turning occasionally.

2. Prepare the grill for the Direct Grilling Method (see page 16). Light the coals. When the briquets become ashen, remove the wings from the marinade, reserving the marinade. Place the wings on an oiled grid over the ashen coals and grill, uncovered, over direct heat for 15 minutes. Turn the wings every 3 minutes and brush with the reserved marinade each time.

3. Transfer the wings to a serving platter and bring to the table with plenty of napkins.

TO COOK INDOORS: Place the marinated wings in a single layer on a foil-covered cookie sheet and bake at 375 degrees for 30 to 35 minutes. Brush once with the reserved marinade after the first 20 minutes.

Turkey Sausages on Sticks

SERVES 6

12   wooden skewers, soaked in water for 30 minutes before use

1½ pounds raw turkey, ground

1   tablespoon chopped fresh chives

1   tablespoon Japanese soy sauce

¼   cup minced red bell peppers

¼   cup minced pitted black olives

1   teaspoon Worcestershire sauce

¼   teaspoon freshly ground black pepper

1. Combine all of the ingredients in a large bowl and mix well.

2. Drain and dry the skewers. Mold about ¼ cup of the turkey mixture into a sausage 4 inches long and fit onto a skewer. Repeat the process with the remaining skewers.

3. Prepare the grill for the Direct Grilling Method (see page 16). Light the coals. When the briquets become ashen, place the skewers on a well-oiled grid over the ashen coals. Grill, uncovered, over direct heat for 7 minutes, turning the skewers carefully every 2 minutes (use a spatula to loosen gently if the sausages stick to the grill).

4. Transfer the skewers with a spatula to a serving platter. Serve immediately with Düsseldorf or Dijon mustard.

TO COOK INDOORS: Prepare the turkey sausage on skewers as directed. Place the skewers on a foil-lined cookie sheet and broil, 6 inches from the heat, turning every 2 minutes until done.

Sliced Duck Breast on Rye Bread

SERVES 6

Duck breasts are not sold in supermarkets, but they are available at specialty butchers or see page 182 for our list of mail-order sources.

1   duck breast, about 1½–1¼ pounds (do not skin or bone)
1   recipe Marinade for Fatty Birds (see page 21)
3   cinnamon sticks for aromatic
12   slices German or Dutch pressed rye bread
1   recipe Caper Mayonnaise (recipe follows)

1. Wash and dry the duck breast. Place it in a large ziplock plastic bag. Add the marinade. Seal the bag, turning a few times to coat the breast. Place the bag in a bowl and marinate for 1 hour at room temperature (or 2 hours in the refrigerator), turning occasionally.

2. Prepare the grill for the Indirect Grilling Method (see page 17). Light the coals. When the briquets become ashen, put the cinnamon sticks in the dripping pan.

3. Remove the duck breast from the marinade, reserving the marinade. Place the breast on an oiled grid, skin side up, over the dripping pan. Grill, covered, with the dampers open, over indirect heat for 40 minutes. The duck breast should be slightly rare and the juices should run pale pink when pierced with a fork.

4. Remove the breast from the grill and let sit at room temperature for 15 minutes or longer. Cut into very thin slices, working against the grain, with a sharp knife.

5. Arrange the room-temperature duck slices on pieces of pressed rye, then trim the rye on the edges so the bread slices are only slightly larger than the duck slices. Top each slice with a dollop of Caper Mayonnaise.

TO COOK INDOORS: Place the duck on an oiled rack in a high-sided pan and roast, uncovered, in a 375-degree oven for 35 to 40 minutes.

Caper Mayonnaise

MAKES 1½ CUPS

1   egg plus 1 egg yolk, at room temperature
3   tablespoons cider vinegar
¼   teaspoon salt
¼   teaspoon freshly ground white pepper
     Large pinch cayenne pepper
½   cup virgin olive oil
½   cup vegetable oil
¼   cup capers, drained and patted dry
¼   cup finely chopped fresh parsley
¼   teaspoon dried basil

1. Place the egg and the yolk in a food processor fitted with the steel blade or a blender. Add the vinegar, salt, white pepper and cayenne pepper. Pulse a few times to combine.

2. Mix the olive and vegetable oils together in a cup with a pouring spout. Turn the food processor on and pour the oil slowly into it in a very thin stream until all has been added and the mayonnaise is thickened. Let sit at room temperature for 5 minutes.

3. Transfer the mayonnaise to a serving bowl and stir in the capers, chopped parsley and basil.

Note: If desired, you can make Caper Mayonaise using 1⅓ cups good-quality store-bought mayonnaise and stir in the cayenne, capers, parsley and basil.

Chicken Legs Stuffed with Apples, Raisins and Rum

SERVES 6

6   chicken legs, thighs attached

STUFFING
¼   cup raisins
3   tablespoons dark rum
4   tablespoons unsalted butter
1   medium-sized onion, minced
1   large Granny Smith or other firm baking apple, peeled, cored and thinly sliced
½   teaspoon ground cinnamon
2   teaspoons sugar
1   cup bread cubes, ½ inch thick
1   cup apple juice

1. Wash and dry the chicken legs. Carefully insert your finger between the flesh and the skin on one of the chicken thighs, making a deep pocket as far down the leg as possible. Repeat with the remaining chicken legs.

2. Prepare the stuffing: Place the raisins in a small bowl and add the rum. Let sit for about 30 minutes, stirring occasionally. Heat the butter in a frying pan until it is sizzling. Add the onion and the apple slices. Sauté lightly, stirring frequently, for about 4 minutes. Remove from the heat.

3. Mix the cinnamon and sugar together and sprinkle over the apple and onion. Add the bread cubes and toss lightly. Stir in the raisin mixture.

4. Divide the stuffing into 6 equal-sized portions and fill the pockets in the chicken legs, pushing the stuffing in as deeply as possible.

5. Prepare the grill for the Direct Grilling Method (see page 16). Light the coals. When the briquets become ashen, brush the legs with the apple juice. Arrange them on a greased grid over the ashen coals, skin side up. Grill, covered, over direct heat for about 24 to 30 minutes, turning every 6 minutes and brushing with apple juice each time. Transfer to a serving platter.

TO COOK INDOORS: Arrange the stuffed legs, skin side up, on a foil-covered cookie sheet and bake for 1 hour at 375 degrees, brushing with apple juice after the first 30 minutes.

Duck Pieces with Beer Barbecue Baste and Grilled Peppers

SERVES 6

2   Long Island ducks, 4½–5 pounds each
1   recipe Marinade for Fatty Birds (see page 21)

BEER BARBECUE BASTE
2   tablespoons Barbecue Sauce (see page 41)
2   tablespoons fresh lime juice
1   tablespoon molasses
1   12-ounce can beer
2   tablespoons brown sugar
½   teaspoon salt
2   fresh or jarred jalapeño peppers, seeded and minced

**4   small green bell peppers, washed, seeded and cut into thirds
    Peanut oil for brushing peppers**

1. Wash and dry the ducks. Cut each in half and remove the legs and
   wings reserving them for another use. Cut each duck half into 4
   pieces of equal width. Place 4 pieces in 1 large ziplock plastic bag
   and 4 in another. Divide the marinade between the 2 bags. Seal each
   bag and turn a few times to coat the duck. Place each bag on a cookie
   sheet and marinate at room temperature for 1 hour (or 2 hours in the
   refrigerator), turning occasionally.

2. Prepare the grill for the Indirect Grilling Method (see page 17). Light
   the coals. Prepare the Beer Barbecue Baste: Combine the barbecue
   sauce, lime juice, molasses, beer, sugar, salt and minced jalapeño
   peppers in a small bowl, mixing well.

3. Remove the duck pieces from the marinade and pat lightly. Prick
   each in several places with a fork and brush each with Beer Barbecue
   Baste.

4. When the coals are ashen, arrange the duck pieces, skin side up,
   over the dripping pan on an ungreased grid. Grill, covered, over indirect heat for 50 minutes, turning every 10 minutes with long-handled tongs and brushing often with the baste. Check the water and
   coals after 30 minutes to see if they need replenishing.

5. Brush each pepper strip with oil and place the peppers on the grid
   directly over the coals on each side of the dripping pan. Grill for 2 to
   3 minutes on each side or until slightly charred. Arrange the duck
   and pepper pieces on a serving platter and bring to the table.

TO COOK INDOORS: Remove the duck pieces from the marinade,
dry and prick in several places with a fork. Brush with the baste. Arrange the pieces on an ungreased rack in a roasting pan with high
sides. Fill the pan with 1/4 inch water. Roast, uncovered, for 15 minutes
at 450 degrees. Turn the duck pieces and reduce the heat to 350 degrees. Continue cooking for 75 minutes—a total of 1½ hours. While the
duck cooks, arrange the pepper strips in a single layer on a foil-covered
cookie sheet. When the duck is done, remove from the oven and turn
on the broiler. Broil the peppers for 2 minutes on each side, until lightly
charred. Arrange the duck pieces and pepper strips on a serving platter
and bring to the table.

Chicken Teriyaki

SERVES 6

This version of chicken teriyaki can be eaten by hand or with tooth-picks. It will work well both as an appetizer and as part of a larger buf-fet. If light Japanese soy sauce and mirin—a sweet Japanese cooking wine made from rice—are not available in your area, see page 182 for our list of mail-order sources.

1   **chicken, about 2½–3 pounds**

MARINADE
1¼ **cups mirin**
¾   **cup plus 1 tablespoon Japanese soy sauce**
2½ **tablespoons sugar**
2   **large cloves garlic, finely chopped**

1. Wash and dry the chicken. Skin it as thoroughly as possible. Cut it into 12 pieces using poultry shears or a Chinese cleaver (or ask your butcher to do it): Cut off the wings and drumsticks, then cut it in half lengthwise. Cut each half into 4 pieces of equal width. Place the chicken pieces in a large ziplock plastic bag.

2. Prepare the marinade: Combine the mirin, soy sauce, sugar and gar-lic in a small bowl, mixing well, and pour the mixture into the bag. Seal the bag and turn several times to coat the chicken. Place the bag in a large bowl at room temperature for 1 hour (or 2 hours in the refrigerator), turning occasionally.

3. Prepare the grill for the Direct Grilling Method (see page 16). Light the coals. When the briquets become ashen, remove the chicken from the marinade, reserving the marinade. Arrange the pieces on an oiled grid over the ashen coals. Grill, covered, over direct heat for 24 minutes, turning the pieces every 6 minutes and brushing them with the reserved marinade each time. Wings should be turned ev-ery 3 minutes.

4. Transfer to a serving platter and bring to the table with napkins and toothpicks.

TO COOK INDOORS: Place the marinated chicken pieces on a foil-covered cookie sheet. Bake at 375 degrees for 45 to 60 minutes. Brush with marinade after the first 20 minutes.

Basket of Breaded Chicken and Turkey Nuggets with Barbecue Sauce

SERVES 8

Either use commercially available cracker crumbs or make your own by placing crackers in a towel and rolling them flat with a rolling pin.

1½ pounds boneless, skinless chicken breast
1½ pounds boneless, skinless turkey breast
1   round Italian bread loaf, 1½–2 pounds with a 9-inch diameter
6   tablespoons unsalted butter
2   cloves garlic, minced
3   eggs, slightly beaten
¾   teaspoon salt
¾   teaspoon freshly ground pepper
¾   teaspoon ground cumin
1½ teaspoons chili powder
4½ cups cracker crumbs
1   recipe Barbecue Sauce (page 41)

1. Wash and dry the chicken and turkey breasts. Remove any visible fat or membrane. Cut the chicken into 1½-by 2-inch pieces. Slice the turkey breast in half horizontally, making 2 pieces, each ½ inch thick. Cut the turkey breast into 1½-by 2-inch pieces.

2. Cut a large circle out of the top of the bread and reserve. Pull the soft white inside out of the bread to make a bowl and use a small, sharp knife to remove the white inside from the cutout bread circle (this will be the basket cover).

3. Melt the butter with the garlic and let sit for 5 minutes. Brush the inside of the bread basket, including the cover, with the garlic butter. Reserve.

4. Beat the eggs with the salt, pepper, cumin and chili powder in a medium-sized bowl. Pour the cracker crumbs onto a flat sheet of foil or wax paper. Dip the chicken and turkey pieces, 1 at a time, into the egg mixture, then into the cracker crumbs, coating each piece.

5. Place the nuggets on a flat plate and let sit for 30 minutes at room temperature to dry out. Prepare the grill for the Direct Grilling Method (see page 16). Light the coals. Preheat the oven to 350 degrees.

6. A few minutes before grilling the nuggets, place the bread basket and cover in the oven and heat for about 10 minutes or until crisp. Heat the Barbecue Sauce in a saucepan over low heat. When the coals become ashen, arrange the nuggets on an oiled grid over the ashen coals and grill, uncovered, over direct heat for about 4 minutes, turning after 2 minutes.

7. Remove the basket from the oven and transfer the hot Barbecue Sauce to a sauceboat. Arrange the grilled nuggets in the bread basket, piling them on top of each other. Place the cover on top and bring to the table with the hot Barbecue Sauce. Serve immediately.

TO COOK INDOORS: Place the vegetable oil in a high-sided pan to a depth of 2 inches. Add a deep-fat thermometer and heat the oil to 375 degrees. Slide 5 or 6 breaded nuggets into the hot oil and fry for about 2 minutes or until browned on all sides. Transfer to paper towels to drain. Fry the remaining nuggets, 6 at a time, until all the nuggets are fried. Arrange the nuggets in the heated garlic bread basket. Serve as directed.

Grilling in 30 Minutes or Less

Grilled food need not take hours to cook. The recipes in this chapter, often by incorporating quicker-cooking parts of birds, are ideal for a quick meal on a busy day.

Grilled Drumsticks with Five-Minute Barbecue Sauce

SERVES 6

BARBECUE SAUCE

1   strip orange zest, 1/4 inch wide, 3 inches long, cut into 3 pieces

1   medium-sized onion, peeled and quartered

2   garlic cloves, peeled

1 1/2 cups tomato juice

1/4   cup fresh orange juice

1/4   cup ketchup

3   tablespoons honey

1   tablespoon Worchestershire sauce

1   tablespoon chili powder

1/2   teaspoon liquid smoke

1/2   teaspoon paprika

1/2   teaspoon red pepper flakes

1/4   teaspoon salt

12   chicken drumsticks

1. Place the orange zest, onion and garlic in a food processor fitted with the steel blade and pulse 3 times or until coarsely chopped. Add the tomato juice, orange juice, ketchup, honey, Worcestershire sauce, chili powder, liquid smoke, paprika, red pepper flakes and salt. Process until smooth.

2. Wash and dry the chicken legs. Place the legs in a glass dish and brush them liberally with sauce on both sides. Cover with plastic wrap and let sit at room temperature for 1 hour (or 2 hours in the refrigerator), turning occasionally. Leave the remaining sauce in the saucepan.

3. Prepare the grill for the Direct Grilling Method (see page 16). Light the coals. When the briquets become ashen, arrange the drumsticks on an oiled grid over the ashen coals. Grill, uncovered, over direct heat for 24 minutes. Turn the drumsticks every 5 to 6 minutes,

brushing each time with the sauce. The legs are done if the juices run clear when the meat is pricked with a fork.

4. A few moments before the drumsticks are finished, reheat the sauce and transfer it to a serving bowl. Arrange the drumsticks on a serving platter and bring to the table with the remaining sauce.

TO COOK INDOORS: Arrange the marinated drumsticks on a foil-lined cookie sheet and bake for 45 to 50 minutes at 375 degrees. Turn once after 20 minutes and brush with the sauce. Serve as directed.

Note: This and all chicken drumstick recipes can be served in 2 toasted garlic bread baskets (see page 42). Arrange the drumsticks in the hollowed-out bread as if they were flowers in a vase.

Turkey Ovals on Heated Rolls

SERVES 6

2   pounds raw turkey, ground
3   tablespoons uncooked oatmeal
1   large egg, slightly beaten
4   scallions, finely minced
½   teaspoon garlic powder
½   teaspoon salt
¼   teaspoon freshly ground black pepper
6   slices red onion, ½ inch thick
1   tablespoon virgin olive oil
6   oval poppyseed rolls
6   tablespoons mayonnaise (or Caper Mayonnaise, see page 90)
6   leaves green or red leaf lettuce

1. Combine the turkey, oatmeal, egg, scallions, garlic powder, salt and pepper in a large bowl and mix well. Divide the mixture into 6 equal portions and form each portion into an oval patty.

2. Prepare the grill for the Direct Grilling Method (see page 16). Light the coals. When the briquets become ashen, place the patties on an

oiled grid over the ashen coals. Cook, covered, over direct heat for 10 to 12 minutes, turning the patties every 5 minutes. (Turkey ovals have a tendency to stick to the grid, even when it is well oiled—if desired, grill each oval on top of a thin slice of orange placed over the grid.)

3. Brush the red onion slices with the olive oil. After the turkey patties have been turned once, arrange the red onions on the grid and grill for 9 minutes, turning every 3 minutes or until lightly charred on both sides.

4. Slice the poppyseed rolls in half and place them on the grid for a moment to warm. Arrange the buns on a platter. Place a turkey oval on the bottom half of each roll and top each patty with a dollop of mayonnaise, a grilled red onion slice and a lettuce leaf. Top each roll and serve immediately with sour pickles and potato chips on the side.

TO COOK INDOORS: Place the turkey ovals on a foil-lined cookie sheet and broil 6 inches from the flame for 10 minutes, turning once after 5 minutes. After turning turkey, add onion slices. Turn the onions after 3 minutes, and cook until the turkey is done.

Blackened Chicken Breasts with Sour Cream and Chives

SERVES 6

6   boneless chicken breast halves, about 5 ounces each, skin removed
1   tablespoon sweet paprika
1   tablespoon onion powder
½   teaspoon salt
½   teaspoon garlic powder
½   teaspoon dried oregano
¼   teaspoon cayenne pepper
½   cup (1 stick) unsalted butter
2   cups sour cream
⅓   cup minced fresh chives

1. Wash and dry the chicken. Place the breasts between 2 wax paper sheets and pound them slightly with a rolling pin to flatten. Combine the paprika, onion powder, salt, garlic powder, oregano and cayenne pepper in a small bowl.

2. Melt the butter. Place the chicken on a plate and brush each side with the melted butter. Sprinkle the herb mixture lightly over both sides of the breasts. Mix the sour cream and chives together in a small bowl.

3. Prepare the grill for the Direct Grilling Method (see page 16). Light the coals. When the briquets become ashen, place the breasts on an oiled grid over the ashen coals. Cook, uncovered, over direct heat for 9 minutes, turning the breasts every 3 minutes until done. Transfer to a serving platter and bring to the table with the sour cream sauce.

TO COOK INDOORS: Place the seasoned breasts on 2 foil-lined cookie sheets. Broil 6 inches from the flame for 9 minutes turning every 3 minutes or until done.

Grilled Stuffed Chicken Turnovers

SERVES 6

The chicken breasts in this delicious recipe are pounded thin, folded in half over a filling of sautéed mushrooms, Swiss cheese and jalapeño peppers and then grilled to perfection.

6   large boneless chicken breast halves, skin removed
2   tablespoons unsalted butter
12   large white mushrooms with stems, each cut into 3–4 lengthwise slices through the cap and stem
6   2- to 3-inch slices Swiss cheese
6   fresh jalapeño peppers, cut in half lengthwise, seeds removed and finely chopped
     Extra chopped jalapeño peppers for garnish (optional)

1. Wash and dry the chicken breast halves. Place each half between 2

sheets of wax paper and pound lightly with a wooden mallet or with a rolling pin to flatten.

2. Heat the butter in a medium-sized saucepan. Add the mushroom slices and sauté over medium heat for about 4 minutes. Allow to cool in the saucepan.

3. Trim the Swiss cheese slices so they cover the right-hand side only of each chicken piece. Place a cheese slice over each chicken breast. Spread the mushroom mixture over the cheese and top with the chopped peppers.

4. Fold the left sides of the chicken breasts over the right sides and flatten each with your hand. Make sure no cheese shows at the seam, or it will melt into the grill. Use toothpicks to close up the chicken if you wish.

5. Prepare the grill for the Direct Grilling Method (see page 16). Light the coals. When the briquets become ashen, place the chicken turnovers on an oiled grid over the ashen coals. Grill, covered, over direct heat for about 9 minutes, turning with a spatula after 4½ minutes. Transfer to a serving platter and serve immediately. Pass extra chopped peppers if desired.

TO COOK INDOORS: Arrange the turnovers on a foil-covered cookie sheet and broil for about 10 minutes, turning after 5 mintues.

Italian Sausage-Stuffed Drumsticks with Smoky Pizza Bread

SERVES 6

12 **chicken drumsticks**

⅔ **pound sweet Italian sausage, removed from casing and mashed with a fork**

Olive oil for brushing drumsticks

Dried oregano for sprinkling on the chicken plus ¼ cup for aromatic

1. Wash and dry the drumsticks. Carefully insert a finger between the flesh and skin on 1 side of each leg to make a pocket without breaking the skin.

2. Push 2 tablespoons of sausage into the drumstick pockets. Brush the legs with oil, then sprinkle them lightly with oregano.

3. Prepare the grill for the Direct Grilling Method (see page 16). Light the coals. When the briquets become ashen, arrange the legs, stuffing side up, on an oiled grid over the ashen coals. Sprinkle the ¼ cup oregano onto the hot coals for aromatic effect. Grill the legs, covered, over direct heat for 24 minutes, turning every 6 minutes and brushing with oil each time. Serve warm with Smoky Pizza Bread (recipe follows).

TO COOK INDOORS: Arrange the stuffed drumsticks on a foil-covered cookie sheet and bake at 375 degrees for 45 to 50 minutes. Brush them with oil after the first 20 minutes.

Smoky Pizza Bread

This accompaniment can be grilled along with the Italian Sausage–Stuffed Drumsticks (recipe above).

3   tablespoons vegetable oil
2   onions, chopped
2   green bell peppers, seeded and chopped
½   teaspoon dried oregano
1   15-inch loaf French bread, halved horizontally
½   cup tomato sauce
4–6 slices mozzarella cheese, or enough to cover both bread halves

1. Heat the oil in 2 medium-sized skillets over medium heat. Add the onions and peppers and sauté until tender, about 5 minutes. Sprinkle the oregano into the pan and stir. Remove from the heat.

2. Place both halves of the bread on the grill, cut side down, for 1 minute—just enough to toast them lightly.

3. Put each bread half, cut side up, on a piece of aluminum foil large enough to wrap all the way around it. Spread ¼ cup tomato sauce on each half. Place the cheese slices over the tomato sauce. Arrange the onions and peppers over the cheese.

4. Wrap the foil loosely around the bread; it should not touch the cheese or vegetable topping. Place the foil packets on the outer edges of the grid for 10 minutes. Serve with Italian Sausage–Stuffed Drumsticks (preceding recipe).

TO COOK INDOORS: Put the bread halves under the broiler 6 inches from the flame for 2 to 3 minutes or until lightly toasted. Turn the broiler off and turn the oven to 350 degrees. Place the bread halves on a foil-covered cookie sheet and spread them with the ingredients as in Step 3 above. Bake for 10 minutes or until the cheese begins to melt.

Drumsticks with Bay Leaves

SERVES 6

This easy dish uses bay leaves and salad dressing, which are on hand in most cupboards. Be sure to pull out the bay leaves before serving. They should not be eaten.

12 **chicken drumsticks**
12 **bay leaves**
½ **cup commercial Italian-style salad dressing**
½ **teaspoon garlic powder**
1 **teaspoon dried oregano**

1. Wash and dry the drumsticks. Carefully insert a finger between the flesh and skin of each drumstick to make a pocket in 1 side without breaking the skin. Insert a whole bay leaf into each drumstick pocket.

2. Combine the salad dressing with the garlic powder and dried ore-

gano in a small bowl. Brush the mixture generously over the drumsticks.

3. Prepare the grill for the Direct Grilling Method (see page 16). Light the coals. When the briquets become ashen, arrange the drumsticks on an oiled grid over the ashen coals. Grill, uncovered, for 24 minutes over direct heat, turning the legs every 6 minutes and brushing with dressing each time.

TO COOK INDOORS: Place the drumsticks on a foil-lined cookie sheet and bake for 45 to 50 minutes at 375 degrees or until crisp and brown. Brush the legs with dressing after the first 20 minutes.

Turkey Chunks with Two Sauces

SERVES 6

This recipe is served with two beautiful fruit sauces—a sweet, golden apricot sauce and a tart kiwifruit sauce. For the most effective presentation, they should be served nouvelle style, with both sauces on the dinner plate underneath the skewers.

Turkey steaks, already cut from the breast, are available in supermarkets. Each one should weigh about 2 ounces, measure 5 by 3 inches and be about 1/2 inch thick.

12   wooden skewers, soaked in water 30 minutes before use
24   dried apricots
3/4   cup brandy
6   kiwifruits
12   turkey steaks cut from the breast, about 1 1/2 to 2 pounds altogether
      Apricot Sauce (recipe follows)
      Kiwifruit Sauce (recipe follows)

1. Put the apricots in a small bowl and sprinkle them with the brandy. Let them sit in the brandy until they are soft, about 30 minutes.

2. Peel the kiwifruits with a small, sharp paring knife: cut off each end

and peel off strips of skin, taking as little flesh as possible. (Do not remove the seeds.) Cut the kiwifruits into quarters.

3. Drain the skewers. Cut each turkey steak in half lengthwise, then in half widthwise to yield 4 pieces per steak. Thread 4 turkey pieces, 2 apricots and 2 kiwifruit quarters onto each skewer.

4. Prepare the grill for the Direct Grilling Method (see page 16). Light the coals. When the briquets become ashen, place the skewers on an oiled grid over the ashen coals. Brush 6 of the skewers liberally with Apricot Sauce and the other 6 with Kiwifruit Sauce. Grill, covered, over direct heat for 9 to 10 minutes, turning the skewers every 3 minutes and brushing with the respective sauces each time.

5. Reheat the Kiwifruit and Apricot Sauces separately in their saucepans. Spoon a small amount of hot Kiwifruit Sauce over one side of a dinner plate. Spoon a small amount of hot Apricot Sauce carefully over the other half of the plate. Use only a little sauce so they will not run into each other. Carefully arrange the skewers across the sauces so 1 end rests on the Kiwifruit Sauce and the other rests on the Apricot Sauce. Serve with the remaining hot sauce in bowls on the table.

TO COOK INDOORS: Place the skewers on a foil-lined cookie sheet and brush with the sauce as above. Broil 6 inches from the flame for 9 to 10 minutes, turning every 3 minutes and brushing with sauce each time. Serve as above.

Kiwifruit Sauce

MAKE 2 CUPS

6   **kiwifruits**
3   **tablespoons unsalted butter**
2   **shallots, minced**
2   **scallions, minced**
1/2 **cup dry white wine**

1. Peel the kiwifruits with a sharp paring knife: cut off each end and peel off strips of skin, taking as little flesh as possible. (Do not remove the seeds.) Cut the kiwifruits into quarters and put them in a food processor fitted with the steel blade. Pulse until coarsely pureed and reserve.

2. Heat the butter in a large saucepan over medium heat. Add the shallots and scallions and sauté for about 3 minutes or until softened. Add the wine and simmer for about 10 minutes or until the volume is reduced by about half.

3. Add the kiwifruit puree and return to a simmer. Heat through and then leave the sauce in the saucepan until ready to serve.

Apricot Sauce

MAKE 2 CUPS

²/₃ **cup dried apricots, cut into quarters**
¹/₂ **cup brandy**
¹/₄ **cup sugar**
5   **teaspoons red wine vinegar**
1¹/₃ **cups canned apricot juice**

1. Put the apricots in a small bowl and sprinkle them with the brandy. Let sit for 30 minutes. Heat the sugar in a medium-sized, heavy-bottomed saucepan, stirring constantly with a wooden spoon, until the sugar melts to a golden brown color.

2. Add the vinegar slowly to prevent spattering. Stir in the apricot juice, mixing well. Add the apricot quarters together with the brandy. Reduce the heat and simmer for 5 minutes, stirring occasionally, until the sauce thickens. Leave the sauce in the saucepan until ready to serve.

Chicken Breasts with Mustard–Crème Fraîche Sauce

SERVES 6

3   tablespoons virgin olive oil
1/2   teaspoon crumbled dried rosemary
3   large whole chicken breasts, wings removed and cut in half lengthwise to yield 6 pieces

MUSTARD–CRÈME FRAÎCHE SAUCE
1 1/2 cups crème fraîche
1   tablespoon Dijon mustard
1/4   teaspoon crumbled dried rosemary

1. Prepare the grill for the Direct Grilling Method (see page 16). Light the coals. Combine olive oil and 1/2 teaspoon rosemary in a small bowl. Wash and dry the chicken and remove any visible fat. Place the chicken breasts on a platter and brush them with the oil-rosemary mixture.

2. Prepare the Mustard–Crème Fraîche Sauce: Combine the crème fraîche, Dijon mustard and 1/4 teaspoon rosemary in a small serving bowl and reserve.

3. When the briquets become ashen, arrange the chicken on an oiled grid, skin side up, over the ashen coals. Grill, covered, over direct heat for about 24 minutes, turning every 4 to 5 minutes.

4. Transfer the chicken to a serving platter and bring to the table with the serving bowl of Mustard–Crème Fraîche Sauce. Serve immediately.

TO COOK INDOORS: Prepare the chicken as directed, brushing with the oil-rosemary mixture. Arrange the breasts on a foil-covered cookie sheet and bake in a 375-degree oven for 25 minutes. Serve as directed with the Mustard–Crème Fraîche Sauce.

Skewer and Rotisserie Grilling

As the barbecue grill grows in popularity, so does the rotisserie—a cooking method that all but guarantees a delicious bird. When you use a rotisserie, you don't have to baste the bird or watch to see whether it is burning in one spot or another. The bird bastes itself as it turns on an automatic spit, and it is never in one position long enough to develop a hot spot.

Serving food on skewers is especially popular with guests. What could be nicer than having your dinner already cut into bite-sized pieces for you?

Chicken Liver Kabobs with Garlic and Mint

SERVES 6

6   wooden skewers, soaked in water for 30 minutes before use

3   cloves garlic, peeled and halved
1/4   cup virgin olive oil
1   teaspoon dried mint, crumbled
1/4   teaspoon salt
1/4   teaspoon freshly ground pepper
18   chicken livers, each halved

1. Combine the garlic, oil, mint, salt and pepper in a food processor fitted with the steel blade and pulse until pureed.

2. Drain the skewers. Thread 6 chicken liver halves onto each skewer. Brush the skewers with the puree.

3. Prepare the grill for the Direct Grilling Method (see page 16). Light the coals. When the briquets become ashen, arrange the skewers on an oiled grid over the ashen coals. Cook, uncovered, over direct heat for 9 minutes, turning every 3 minutes.

4. Transfer to a serving platter and serve immediately.

TO COOK INDOORS: Place the skewers on a foil-covered cookie sheet. Broil 6 inches from the flame for 9 minutes, turning the livers every 3 minutes.

Chicken Kabobs with Orange Butter

SERVES 6

6	wooden skewers, soaked in water for 30 minutes before use
	Orange Butter (recipe follows)
6	medium-sized sweet potatoes, peeled and cut into 1½-inch chunks

MARINADE

4	tablespoons corn oil
1¼	cups fresh orange juice
½	teaspoon ground cloves
½	teaspoon ground allspice
½	teaspoon ground cinnamon
1	large bay leaf

1½	pounds boneless and skinless chicken breasts
3	navel oranges, cut into ½-inch slices (about 15 pieces)
2	green bell peppers, cut into 2-inch chunks

1. Remove the Orange Butter from the refrigerator so it can come to room temperature. Put the sweet potato chunks in a saucepan, cover with water and heat to a boil. Reduce the heat and simmer for 25 minutes or until the potatoes can be pierced easily with a fork. Drain them and let cool.

2. Prepare the marinade: Combine the oil, orange juice, cloves, allspice, cinnamon and bay leaf in a small bowl. Wash and dry chicken breasts. Cut into 1¼-inch chunks and place them in a large ziplock plastic bag. Add the marinade. Seal the bag and turn several times to coat the chicken. Put the bag in a large bowl and marinate for 1 hour at room temperature (or 2 hours in the refrigerator), turning occasionally.

3. Remove the chicken from the marinade, reserving the marinade. Thread chicken pieces onto the skewers alternately with the orange slices, peppers and sweet potato chunks.

4. Prepare the grill for the Direct Grilling Method (see page 16). Light the coals. When the briquets become ashen, place the skewers on an oiled grid over the ashen coals. Grill, covered, over direct heat for 12 minutes, turning every 4 to 5 minutes and brushing with marinade each time.

5. Transfer the skewers to a serving platter and bring to the table with the Orange Butter. Guests should spread about 4 teaspoons of Orange Butter onto each kabob, then remove them from the skewer.

TO COOK INDOORS: Arrange the kabobs on a foil-lined cookie sheet and broil 6 inches from the flame for 12 minutes, turning after 6 minutes. Serve as directed.

Orange Butter

MAKES ½ CUP

½ cup unsalted butter, at room temperature
2 tablespoons light brown sugar
1 tablespoon fresh orange juice
½ teaspoon grated orange zest

1. Combine the softened butter with the sugar, orange juice and zest in a small bowl, mixing well. Serve with Chicken Kabobs.

Turkey and Fig Kabobs with Hot Fig Sauce

SERVES 6

12   wooden skewers, soaked in water for 30 minutes before use

12   turkey steaks, cut from the breast (about 1½ to 2 pounds altogether)

1   recipe Marinade for Lean Birds (see page 21)

HOT FIG SAUCE

1   17-ounce jar figs in heavy syrup

½   cup white wine

½   cup sugar

48   large red grapes, preferably seedless

24   dried figs (or substitute 12 fresh figs, halved)

¾   cup Marsala or Madeira

1. Cut each turkey steak in half lengthwise to measure 2½ by 3 inches. Place the turkey steaks in a ziplock plastic bag. Pour the marinade into the bag. Seal the bag and turn it several times to coat the turkey. Place the bag on a cookie sheet and marinate at room temperature for 1 hour (or 2 hours in the refrigerator), turning occasionally.

2. Prepare the Hot Fig Sauce: Drain the jarred figs, reserving syrup. Place the figs in a food processor fitted with the steel blade and pulse until coarsely chopped. Pour the chopped figs into a saucepan, along with the reserved fig syrup, white wine and sugar. Bring the mixture to a boil, reduce the heat and simmer, uncovered, for 20 minutes, stirring occasionally. Allow to cool but do not remove from the saucepan.

3. Drain the skewers. Thread 2 grapes onto 1 end of a skewer. Then thread a turkey strip followed by a fig followed by a second turkey strip and a second fig. Finish with 2 grapes. Repeat this process with the remaining skewers, putting 2 turkey strips, 2 dried figs and 4 grapes on each. Brush the skewers liberally with the Hot Fig Sauce on each side.

4. Prepare the grill for the Direct Grilling Method (see page 16). Light the coals. When the briquets become ashen, set the skewers on an oiled grid over the ashen coals. Grill, covered, over direct heat for 9 to 10 minutes, turning the skewers every 3 minutes and brushing with the fig sauce each time. Reheat the fig sauce and spoon into a sauceboat. Arrange the skewers on a serving platter and bring to the table with the Hot Fig Sauce.

TO COOK INDOORS: Place the skewers on a foil-covered cookie sheet and broil 6 inches from the flame for 9 minutes. Turn the skewers every 3 minutes, brushing with fig sauce each time.

Chicken and Livers Yakitori

SERVES 6

12   wooden skewers, soaked in water for 30 minutes before use

4   large boneless and skinless chicken breast halves
12   chicken livers

MARINADE

1   cup Japanese soy sauce
½   cup dry white wine
2   tablespoons sugar
½   teaspoon garlic powder
½   teaspoon ground ginger
¼   teaspoon cayenne pepper
2   small Japanese white or purple eggplants, unpeeled and cut into 24 ½-inch rounds (or substitute 2 small regular eggplants, peeled and cut into 1½-inch chunks)
1   6½-ounce whole water chestnuts, drained (about 24 water chestnuts)
4   small green bell peppers, each cut into 6 large squares to yield 24 pieces

1. Wash and dry the chicken breasts and livers. Cut each breast half into 6 1- to 1½-inch pieces. Cut each liver in half. Place the breast and liver pieces in a large ziplock plastic bag.

2. Prepare the marinade: Combine the soy sauce, wine, sugar, garlic, ginger and cayenne pepper in a small bowl. Pour the marinade into the plastic bag. Seal the bag and turn it several times to coat the chicken. Place the bag in a bowl and marinate at room temperature for 1 hour (or 2 hours in the refrigerator), turning occasionally.

3. Remove the chicken and livers from the marinade, reserving the marinade. Drain the skewers. Thread the skewers: put 2 of each ingredient (chicken pieces, liver pieces, eggplant, water chestnuts and peppers) on each skewer, sliding them on alternately.

4. Prepare the grill for the Direct Grilling Method (see page 16). Light the coals. When the briquets become ashen, place the skewers on an oiled grid over the ashen coals. Grill, uncovered, over direct heat for 8 to 9 minutes, turning and brushing with the reserved marinade every 3 minutes.

5. Transfer the skewers to a serving platter and serve immediately.

TO COOK INDOORS: Place the skewers on a foil-lined cookie sheet and broil 6 inches from the flame for 9 minutes, turning once after 3 minutes and brushing liberally with marinade.

Turkey Strips with Spicy Peanut Sauce

SERVES 6

This recipe is similar to an Indonesian sate, but it uses turkey strips threaded onto skewers instead of pork chunks. Since the marinade is used in the sauce, it is made without oil. This recipe uses turkey steaks, which are availble in supermarkets. Each turkey steak has been cut from the breast, should weigh slightly over 2 ounces and should measure 5 by 3 inches and be ½ inch thick.

12   wooden skewers, soaked in water for 30 minutes before use

12   turkey steaks (about 1¾ to 2 pounds altogether)

MARINADE
¼   cup Japanese soy sauce
½   cup chicken broth
3   tablespoons brown sugar
½   teaspoon ground ginger
½   teaspoon garlic powder
¼   cup oil for brushing the turkey strips
1   recipe Spicy Peanut Sauce (recipe follows)

1. Cut each turkey steak in half lengthwise, so that each piece measures 2½ by 3 inches. Place the halves in a large ziplock plastic bag.

2. Prepare the marinade: Combine the soy sauce, chicken broth, sugar, ginger and garlic powder in a small bowl, mixing well. Pour the marinade into the bag. Seal the bag and turn several times to coat the turkey. Place the bag in a large bowl and marinate for 1 hour at room temperature (or 2 hours in the refrigerator), turning occasionally.

3. Remove the turkey from the marinade, reserving the marinade for use in the sauce. Drain the skewers. Thread the skewers with 2 turkey pieces per skewer.

4. Prepare the grill for the Direct Grilling Method (see page 16). Light the coals. When the briquets have become ashen, arrange the skewers on an oiled grid over the ashen coals and brush with the oil. Grill, uncovered, over direct heat for 9 to 10 minutes, turning the skewers every 3 minutes and brushing them with oil each time.

5. Arrange the skewers on a serving platter and bring to the table. Pass with Spicy Peanut Sauce.

TO COOK INDOORS: Arrange the skewers on a foil-covered cookie sheet and broil 6 inches from the flame for 9 to 10 minutes, turning the skewers every 3 minutes and brushing with oil. Serve as directed.

Spicy Peanut Sauce

MAKES 2 CUPS

1   cup roasted, unsalted peanuts
3   tablespoons unsalted butter
1   medium onion, minced
3   cloves garlic, minced
3/4 teaspoon curry powder
1/2 teaspoon red pepper flakes, or more to taste
1 1/2 cups reserved marinade (see above), or add enough water to
     measure 1 1/2 cups liquid

1. Place the peanuts in a food processor fitted with the steel blade and
   pulse until coarsely ground. Reserve. Heat the butter in a medium-
   sized saucepan, add the onion and garlic and sauté for 3 minutes
   over medium heat.

2. Add the ground peanuts, curry powder, pepper flakes and marinade. Bring to a boil, reduce the heat and simmer for 8 to 10 minutes, stirring occasionally. Let sit in the saucepan until ready to serve.

Murghi Malai Kabab
(Indian Chicken Kabobs)

SERVES 6

When foodwriter Colleen Taylor Sen visited India with her husband,
Ashish Sen, they had dinner at Moti Mahal, one of India's foremost restaurants. The food was so extraordinary that the Sens managed to
wheedle the recipe for one of the restaurant's specialties from the
owner, Kundan Lal Gujral. Although the dish is made in a tandoor—a
large clay oven buried in the ground—the Sens adapted it for use on the
barbecue. "Don't be surprised by the Velveeta in this recipe," Colleen
explains. "The native cheese used in India is unavailable in this country, and Velveeta is similar enough to substitute."

12 wooden skewers, soaked in water for 30 minutes before use

3   boneless and skinless chicken breast halves
1   tablespoon finely minced garlic
1   1-inch piece peeled fresh gingerroot, very finely minced
1   teaspoon fresh lemon juice
1/2 teaspoon salt
3   ounces Velveeta cheese
1/4 cup heavy cream
1   tablespoon finely chopped fresh cilantro (coriander)
1   large jalapeño pepper, seeded and finely chopped

1. Cut each chicken breast half into 4 strips, about 3 to 4 inches long. Combine the garlic, ginger, lemon juice and salt in a small bowl. Rub the chicken strips with this mixture and let sit for 30 minutes.

2. Combine the Velveeta, cream, cilantro and chilies in a food processor fitted with the steel blade and pulse a few times to chop finely. Pour this mixture into a large ziplock plastic bag. Take the chicken strips out of the small bowl and add to bag. Seal the bag and marinate for 1 hour at room temperature (or 2 hours in the refrigerator), turning occasionally.

3. Drain the skewers. Thread 1 chicken strip on each of the 12 drained skewers (see illustration, page 116).

4. Prepare the grill for the Direct Grilling Method (see page 16). Light the coals. When the briquets become ashen, place the skewers on an oiled grid over the ashen coals. Grill, covered, over direct heat for 15 to 20 minutes, turning every 4 or 5 minutes.

5. Transfer to a serving platter and serve immediately.

TO COOK INDOORS: Arrange the twice-marinated chicken on a foil-covered cookie sheet and bake in a 400-degree oven for 20 minutes, turning the strips once after 10 minutes.

Spit-Grilled Partridge with Prune Sauce

SERVES 6

6   partridge, about 1 pound each
1   recipe Marinade for Lean Birds (see page 21)

PRUNE SAUCE
½   pound dried pitted prunes, quartered
2½ cups water
¼   cup fresh lemon juice
¼   cup sugar
2   tablespoons unsalted butter
4   teaspoons all-purpose flour
½   cup dry white wine
⅛   teaspoon salt
¼   teaspoon ground cinnamon
½   cup sour cream, at room temperature

1   cup prunes for platter garnish (optional)
1   handful parsley sprigs for platter garnish (optional)

1. Wash and dry the partridge. Place 3 partridge in each of 2 ziplock plastic bags. Divide the marinade between the bags. Seal the bags and turn several times to coat the partridge. Place the bags on a cookie sheet and marinate at room temperature for 1 hour (or 2 hours in the refrigerator), turning occasionally.

2. Prepare the grill for the Indirect Grilling Method (see page 17). Light the coals. Prepare the Prune Sauce: Place the pitted prunes, water, lemon juice and sugar in a saucepan and heat to a simmer. Simmer for 15 to 20 minutes or until the prunes are soft. Drain the prunes, reserving both the prunes and the liquid. The liquid should measure about 1 cup. Add water if necessary to make the full quantity.

3. Heat the butter in a medium-sized saucepan. Add the flour and stir with a whisk until the flour is incorporated. Immediately add the white wine and 1 cup prune liquid, stirring constantly with the whisk until the mixture thickens.

4. Remove the pan from the heat and stir in the salt and cinnamon. Let cool slightly, then add the sour cream, whisking to combine. Stir in the reserved prunes and set the sauce aside in the saucepan until ready to use.

5. Remove the partridge from the marinade, reserving the marinade. Thread the partridge on a rotisserie spit, truss each with strong twine, then use the spit tongs to secure each in place. When the briquets become ashen, attach the spit to the rotisserie according to the manufacturer's directions.

6. Turn the rotisserie on and let run for 35 to 40 minutes. To test for doneness, insert a fork into the partridge thighs; if the juices run clear, the partridge are done. Using oven mitts, remove the partridge from the spit and arrange on a serving platter.

7. Reheat the sauce, but do not let it boil. Spoon it into a serving bowl. Bring the sauce to the table with the platter of partridge. Garnish the platter with whole prunes and parsley sprigs if desired.

TO COOK INDOORS: Marinate the partridge as above and prepare the sauce as directed. Arrange the partridge, breast side up, on a foil-lined cookie sheet. Place them in a 375-degree oven for 25 to 30 minutes or until they test done (see above). Brush them with marinade after 15 minutes. Serve as directed above.

Ducks on a Spit with Lime Marmalade Baste and Chilled Mango Puree

SERVES 4

2   Long Island ducks, about 4 to 5 pounds each
1   recipe Marinade for Fatty Birds (see page 21)
2   cups lime marmalade
¼   cup water
4   ripe mangoes
4   limes, quartered

1. Prepare the grill for the Indirect Grilling Method (see page 17). Light the coals. Wash and dry the ducks, removing any visible fat. Place each duck in a large ziplock plastic bag and divide the marinade between the bags. Seal the bags and turn several times to coat the ducks. Place the bags on a cookie sheet for 1 hour at room temperature (or 2 hours in the refrigerator), turning occasionally.

2. Combine the lime marmalade and water in a small saucepan over medium heat, stirring with a wire whisk occasionally, until the marmalade has melted and the mixture is smooth. Set aside until ready to grill. Peel the mangoes, remove the mango flesh and discard the pit. Place the mango flesh in a food processor fitted with the steel blade and pulse several times until pureed. Spoon the puree into a serving bowl, cover and refrigerate until ready to serve.

3. Remove the ducks from the marinade and prick each one all over its body with a fork. Place 8 lime quarters in each cavity. Thread the ducks on a rotisserie spit, trussing each with strong twine, then use the spit tongs to secure each in place. When the briquets become ashen, attach the spit to the rotisserie according to the manufacturer's directions.

4. Turn the rotisserie on and let run for 2 hours or until the ducks have turned a golden brown color. Place a large empty can near the grill so you can carefully ladle fat out of the drip pan as it accumulates. Because of the fatty nature of the duck, be aware of flare-up possibilities—have a pan of water available to sprinkle on the fire if necessary. Try not to leave the duck unattended.

5. During the last hour of grilling, brush the ducks every 15 minutes with the lime marmalade basting sauce. Test for doneness by inserting a fork into the deepest part of the thigh; if the juices run clear, the ducks are done. If the juices run pink, the ducks need more grilling.

6. Using oven mitts, remove the ducks from the spit and place them on a serving board in the kitchen. Remove the limes from the cavities and discard. Let sit for 15 minutes, then use poultry shears to cut the ducks first in half, then into quarters. Arrange the duck pieces on a serving platter and bring to the table with the mango puree.

TO COOK INDOORS: Prepare the duck as above. Preheat the oven to 450 degrees. Place the duck on a rack in a roasting pan, with ¼ inch of water in the pan bottom. Put in 450-degree oven for 15 minutes, reduce the temperature to 350 degrees and cook an additional 90 minutes. The duck is done when it is golden colored and the joints move freely.

Spit-Grilled Quail with Pistachio Butter

SERVES 4

8   quail, 3½ ounces each
1   recipe Marinade for Lean Birds (see page 21)

PISTACHIO BUTTER
1   cup shelled pistachio nuts
½   cup stemmed fresh parsley
3   tablespoons corn oil
4   slices white bread (use whole bakery bread if possible), crusts removed

1. Wash and dry the quail. Place 4 quail in each of 2 large ziplock plastic bags and divide the marinade between the bags. Seal the bags and turn several times to coat the quail. Place each bag in a large bowl and marinate for 1 hour at room temperature (or 2 hours in the refrigerator), turning occasionally.

2. Prepare the grill for the Direct Grilling Method (see page 16). Light the coals. Prepare the Pistachio Butter: Put the pistachio nuts and parsley into the food processor fitted with the steel blade. Turn on the motor and puree, drizzling the oil through the feed tube in a slow, steady stream until everything is pureed.

3. Remove the quail from the marinade. Place 1 quail on the counter with the cavity facing you. Use your fingers to open a pocket between the skin and flesh on either side of the breastbone. The skin is very fragile, so you will need to work slowly and carefully. Repeat this process with the remaining quail.

4. Pat ½ teaspoon Pistachio Butter under the skin on each side of the breast bone, using 1 teaspoon per bird. Thread the quail on a rotisserie spit, truss each with strong twine, then use the spit tongs to secure them in place. When the briquets become ashen, attach the spit to the rotisserie according to manufacturer's directions.

5. Turn the rotisserie motor on and grill the quail over the ashen coals for 25 minutes. The quail are done when their joints move freely and the juices run clear when meat is pricked with a fork. Using oven mitts, remove the quail from the spit and arrange them on a serving platter.

6. While the quail are grilling, toast the bread. Spread each piece with extra Pistachio Butter, then cut slices crosswise into triangles, making 8 pieces altogether. Arrange the toast triangles on a serving platter. Place a quail on top of each triangle and bring the platter to the table.

TO COOK INDOORS: Marinade the quail and stuff them as directed with Pistachio Butter. Arrange them on a foil-lined cookie sheet and roast for about 15 minutes at 375 degrees. The quail are done when the joints move easily and the juices run clear when the meat is pricked with a fork.

Goose on a Spit

SERVES 4 TO 6

Goose grilled on the rotisserie is unbelievably delicious, but takes constant care. Never leave it unattended while it rotates on the spit—it is so fatty that flare-ups can and will occur at any time. If you decide to spit-grill a goose—and the succulent, rich, golden brown results are more than worth it—place a bowl of water near the grill so you will have something to sprinkle on the coals when they flare up. Keep a pair of oven mitts handy as well.

You will note that the recipe calls for crème de cassis. This is a sweet French liqueur made from black currants.

▗▖

1   **goose, about 9 pounds**
     Double recipe Marinade for Fatty Birds (see page 21)

WALNUT PRUNE STUFFING

½   **cup minced walnuts**

20   **dried pitted prunes, chopped**

4   **tablespoons crème de cassis**

⅓   **cup breadcrumbs**

½   **teaspoon ground ginger**

8   **whole cloves**

1   **onion**

6   **pitted prunes**

The most elaborate goose ever prepared was served in San Francisco in 1860 by William Chapman Ralston, an ultrarich California rancher. Chapman, whose dinner parties were legendary, outdid himself on one occasion. He served goose stuffed with snipe stuffed with linnet stuffed with hummingbirds, which in turn had been stuffed with whole almonds. The goose, which was cooked in sandlewood smoke, had been marinating in wine for six days before the party.

1. Wash and dry the goose, removing all visible fat. Put the goose and the marinade in a large ziplock plastic bag. Seal the bag and turn several times to coat the goose. Place the bag on a cookie sheet and marinate for 1 hour at room temperature (or 2 hours in the refrigerator), turning occasionally.

2. Prepare the grill for the Indirect Grilling Method (see page 17). Light the coals. Prepare the Walnut Prune Stuffing: Combine the walnuts, prunes, crème de cassis, breadcrumbs and ginger in a medium-sized bowl.

3. Remove the goose from the marinade. Place it on the counter with the cavity facing you. Using your fingers, carefully separate the skin from the flesh on each side of the breastbone, creating a pocket for the stuffing. Make the pockets as deep as possible, going as far back as the top of the drumstick. Be careful not to tear the skin.

4. Spoon the stuffing under the skin on both sides of the breastbone, patting it down and covering as much of the flesh as possible. Smooth the skin over the stuffing. Truss the goose with kitchen twine to prevent the stuffing from falling out on the rotisserie. Stick the cloves into the onion and place it inside the goose cavity together with the 6 prunes. Prick the goose body and legs all over with fork. Do not prick the stuffed breast.

5. Thread the goose on a rotisserie spit, securing it tightly with spit tongs. When the briquets become ashen, attach the spit to the rotisserie according to the manufacturer's directions and turn the motor on. Bring a large empty coffee can, a large spoon and oven mitts to

the rotisserie. The goose will drip an enormous amount of fat into the dripping pan, so you will need to skim fat often with the spoon, transferring it to the coffee can.

6. Grill the goose for 3 hours on the rotisserie. If the breast skin seems to be getting too well done because of occasional flare-ups, stop the rotisserie and tie a small piece of foil over the breast skin with kitchen twine. The goose will be golden brown when done, and the joints will move freely. The juices will run clear when the thigh is pricked with a fork.

7. Using oven mitts, remove the goose from the spit and place it on a cutting board in the kitchen. Let the goose sit for 20 to 30 minutes before carving. Carve, arrange the slices of goose on a serving platter and bring to the table.

TO COOK INDOORS: Prepare the goose as directed, spooning the stuffing under the skin. Place the goose on a rack in a roasting pan, breast side down, and press a sheet of foil over the goose. Roast the goose in a 400-degree oven for 1 hour, pouring off the fat that collects in the bottom of the pan every 30 minutes. Lower the heat to 350 degrees. Using oven mitts, turn the goose over with your hands and discard the foil. Roast the goose, uncovered and breast side up, for another hour, pouring off the fat every 30 minutes. After 2 hours, remove the goose from the oven and prick it all over with a fork. Return it to the oven and roast for 1 more hour—a total of 3 hours altogether. Continue roasting until the goose is golden brown all over with crispy skin. The leg joints will move freely and the juices will run clear when the thigh is pricked with a fork. Transfer the goose to a cutting board and let sit for 30 minutes before carving. Transfer it to a serving platter and carve it at the table.

The Water-Smoked Grill

Water smoking is very easy to do if you own a small metal smoker. Fill the charcoal pan at the bottom with charcoal, fill the water pan in the middle with hot water and throw a handful of wood chips onto the charcoal when it gets good and hot (for a more detailed description, see page 18). The food—a chicken, turkey or pheasant, for example—is simply set on top of the smoker. You won't ever need to fuss with a brine, a marinade or a salt rub. In just a few hours, you will have a smoky-flavored delicacy.

The skin on large poultry that has been smoked longer than two hours can toughen during smoking and is unpleasant to eat, so remove it before serving.

Smoked Honey-Mustard Chicken with Noodle Pudding

SERVES 6

1   **chicken, about 3¹/₂ pounds, cut in half**
6   **tablespoons honey**
2   **tablespoons coarse-ground mustard with seeds**
2   **cups hickory chips, soaked in water for 30 minutes before use**
¹/₂   **cup whole cloves for aromatic**
1¹/₂ **cups honey**
     Noodle Pudding (recipe follows)

1. Fill the smoker's charcoal pan ³/₄ full with briquets. Light the coals. Wash and dry the chicken halves, removing any visible fat. Mix the 6 tablespoons of honey and the mustard together in a small dish and spread the mixture over the chicken on all sides.

2. When the coals are partly ashen, drain the hickory chips and place them over the charcoal. Fill the water pan with boiling water and add the cloves to the water.

3. Place the chicken halves on an ungreased grid in the smoker. Cover the smoker. Smoke for 70 minutes without turning, checking every 30 minutes to see if more water or coals are needed. Test for doneness by inserting a fork into the chicken. If the juices run clear, the chicken is done; if they run pink, it needs more time in the smoker.

4. Transfer the chicken halves to a cutting board and let stand for 5 minutes. Cut off the wings and legs with poultry shears or a Chinese cleaver. Cut each half into 4 pieces of equal width. Pour the 1¹/₂ cups honey into a sauceboat.

5. Arrange the chicken pieces on a serving platter. Bring to the table with the honey and Noodle Pudding.

TO COOK INDOORS: Marinate chicken in a solution of 1 cup water and ¹/₂ cup liquid smoke for 1 hour at room temperature. Remove from marinade and rub the chiken halves on all sides with honey-mustard mixture above. Arrange the halves on a foil-covered cookie sheet. Bake at 375 degrees for 1 hour, brushing once with honey after 30 minutes.

Noodle Pudding

SERVES 9

1   12-ounce bag medium-width noodles
4   tablespoons unsalted butter
3   apples, peeled and thinly sliced
½   cup golden raisins
1   teaspoon ground cinnamon
1½ cups small-curd cottage cheese
4   eggs, slightly beaten
½   teaspoon grated lemon zest
½   cup milk
½   cup sugar

1. Bring a large saucepan of water to a boil. Slide the noodles into the boiling water and cook for 6 minutes or until done. Drain immediately and reserve.

2. Heat the butter in a frying pan until bubbly. Add the apple slices and sauté for 4 minutes until tender, stirring occasionally. Stir in the raisins and cinnamon and reserve.

3. Preheat the oven to 350 degrees. In a large bowl, combine the cottage cheese, eggs, lemon zest, milk and sugar. Mix well. Add the noodles and apple slices to the bowl and toss together. Spoon the mixture into a greased 9- by 9-inch pan.

4. Bake for 45 minutes or until crusty on top and firm in the center. Cut into 3-inch squares. Serve hot, warm or cold.

Smoked Mallard with Homemade Plum Sauce

SERVES 6

The plum wafers referred to in this recipe are dried plums eaten by Asian children as readily as American children eat gumdrops. They are wrapped in colorful paper and sold at Oriental food stores. If you can't find them, see page 182 for our list of mail-order sources. If you're really stuck, substitute 2 tablespoons ketchup for the plum wafer. Don't worry about authenticity—the Chinese also invented ketchup.

3   **mallards, about 2½ pounds each**
4   **large chunks mesquite, about 2½ by 5 inches, soaked in water for 1 hour before use**

PLUM SAUCE

1   **plum wafer**
¼   **cup white wine vinegar**
½   **cup water**
⅓   **cup canned pineapple juice**
¼   **cup sugar**
2   **tablespoons Japanese soy sauce**
2   **cloves garlic, minced**

1. Examine the mallards for pinfeathers, removing any you find with tweezers or needlenose pliers. Wash and dry the mallards and cut each in half with poultry shears or a Chinese cleaver. Remove the wings and store them in a plastic bag in the freezer for another use.

2. Fill the smoker's charcoal pan ¾ full with briquets. Drain the mesquite and place it on top of the charcoal. Light the coals. When the briquets are partly ashen, fill the water pan with boiling water. Arrange the duck halves on an ungreased grid and cover the smoker. Smoke for 1 hour and 45 minutes, checking every 45 minutes to see if more water or charcoal is needed. The duck is done if the juices run clear when the meat is pricked with a fork.

3. While the duck is smoking, prepare the Plum Sauce: Soak the plum wafer in the wine vinegar in a small bowl for 15 minutes or until the wafer dissolves completely. Combine the water, pineapple juice, sugar, soy sauce and garlic in another bowl. Stir the wafer-vinegar mixture into the pineapple juice mixture and let stand for 15 minutes, then serve with duck.

TO COOK INDOORS: Arrange the mallards, skin side up, on a foil-lined cookie sheet and brush them all over with olive oil. Bake at 350 degrees for 45 to 50 minutes, brushing with oil every 20 minutes. Serve as directed above.

Smoked Long Island Duck with Mandarin Orange Sauce

SERVES 4 TO 6

2   **Long Island ducks, about 5 pounds each**
4   **tablespoons honey**
4   **tablespoons cider vinegar**
½   **teaspoon ground ginger**
4   **large chunks mesquite, about 2½ by 5 inches each, soaked in water for 1 hour before use**
2   **tablespoons grated orange zest**

Mandarin Orange Sauce can be made in advance and refrigerated, then reheated before serving.

MANDARIN ORANGE SAUCE

1   **11-ounce can mandarin orange segments, with liquid**
3   **tablespoons unsalted butter**
2   **shallots, minced**
¼   **cup chicken broth**
¼   **teaspoon salt**
½   **teaspoon minced orange zest**
3   **tablespoons sugar**

1. Wash and dry the ducks. Half fill a large soup kettle with water. Bring the water to a boil, reduce the heat to a simmer and add the honey, vinegar and ginger.

2. Lower 1 duck into the simmering water, breast side down, and simmer for 3 minutes. Turn the duck breast side up and simmer for another 3 minutes. Carefully lift the duck from the water and place it on a platter to drain. Repeat with the remaining duck.

3. Cut a 3-foot piece of string and tie 1 end around the duck wing close to the body. Tie the other end of the string around the remaining wing. Hang the duck over a shower nozzle with a dripping pan underneath. Repeat with the other duck, hanging it from a different faucet with a dripping pan underneath. Let the ducks hang for 1 hour, then take them down and dry with kitchen towels.

4. Cut the ducks in half. Remove the wings and place them in a plastic bag in the freezer for another use. Fill the smoker's charcoal pan ¾ full with briquets. Drain the mesquite and place it on top of the coals. Light the coals. When the briquets are partly ashen, fill the water pan with boiling water and add 2 tablespoons grated orange zest to the pan. Arrange the duck halves on an ungreased grid and cover the smoker. Smoke for 1 hour and 45 minutes, checking every 45 minutes to see if additional charcoal or water is needed. The duck is done if the juices run clear when the meat is pricked with a fork.

5. While the duck is smoking, prepare the Mandarin Orange Sauce: Puree the mandarin orange segments with their juice in a food processor fitted with the steel blade. Set aside. Heat the butter and sauté the shallots over medium heat until soft, about 3 to 5 minutes.

6. Add the mandarin orange puree and the chicken broth to the shallot mixture. Simmer over medium heat for 10 to 15 minutes or until slightly thick. Stir in the salt and the ½ teaspoon orange zest and set aside.

7. In a separate saucepan, heat the sugar over low heat until it is melted. Cook it slowly, stirring constantly, until it turns a golden brown. Remove from the heat immediately and slowly add the orange sauce to the sugar, taking care to prevent spatters. Mix well.

8. Remove the ducks from the smoker and take off all their skin. Cut each duck into 10 pieces with poultry shears or a Chinese cleaver: Remove the drumsticks, then cut each duck half into 4 pieces of equal width. Reheat the Mandarin Orange Sauce.

9. Arrange the 20 duck pieces on a platter and serve with the hot Mandarin Orange Sauce.

TO COOK INDOORS: Poach and hang the ducks as directed. Cut the ducks in half, but do not remove the wings as the duck will not be smoked. Place the duck halves, skin side up, on a rack set in a high-sided, foil-lined roasting pan. Add ½ inch water to the pan. Roast for 45 minutes to 1 hour at 425 degrees. Reduce the heat to 375 degrees, turn the halves over and roast for another 45 minutes, uncovered. There is no need to peel the ducks as they are not smoked.

Let the ducks cool a few moments, then cut each one into 12 pieces. Using poultry shears or a Chinese cleaver, cut off the wings and legs and place them on a platter. Cut each duck half into 4 pieces as directed. Arrange the 24 duck pieces on a serving platter and serve with hot Mandarin Orange Sauce.

Smoked Honeyed Chicken with Kumquat Slivers

SERVES 6

This recipe calls for star anise and oyster sauce—two ingredients available in Chinese specialty food shops. If you can't find them, see page 182 for our list of mail-order sources. Star anise is an aromatic seed unrelated to anise, but the two share an essential oil. Star anise grows in an eight-pointed cluster shaped like a star. Oyster sauce is based on oyster extract, but has a mild, appetizing, meatlike flavor and aroma.

If you do not have a smoker, you will be pleasantly surprised by the indoor preparation provided here. The chicken is marinated in a mixture of natural liquid smoke and water, which gives it a delicious flavor.

Liquid smoke is put on the market in two ways—as a chemical and as a natural distillation of smoke. Be sure to choose the product marked "natural." Although the marinating liquid is black, the finished dish is quite attractive.

3   small chickens, about 2½ pounds each, halved
6   tablespoons honey
4   chunks mesquite, about 4 by 2½ inches each, soaked in water
     for 1 hour before use
6   star anise seeds
6   tablespoons oyster sauce
8   jarred kumquats

1. Fill the smoker's charcoal pan ¾ full with briquets. Light the coals. Wash and dry the chickens, removing all visible fat. Brush the birds with the honey and reserve. When the briquets are partly ashen, drain the mesquite and place it over the charcoal. Fill the water pan with boiling water and add the star anise to the water.

2. Place the chicken halves on an ungreased grid and cover the smoker. Smoke for about 1 hour and 15 minutes, checking every 30 to 45 minutes to see if more water or coals are needed. Test the chickens for doneness by inserting a fork into the meat. If the juices run clear, the chicken is done; if they run pink, it needs more time in the smoker.

3. Place the chickens on a tray and brush each with the oyster sauce. Take 6 kumquats from the jar and cut each into long, thin slivers. Place the chicken halves on a serving platter and garnish with the kumquat slivers. Serve hot or cold.

TO COOK INDOORS: Combine 1 cup natural liquid smoke with 2 cups water. Place 2 of the chicken halves in each of 3 large ziplock plastic bags and pour 1 cup marinade into each bag. Seal the bags and turn several times to coat the chicken. Place the bags on cookie sheets and marinate for 1 hour at room temperature (or 2 hours in the refrigerator), turning the bags often.

Remove the chickens from the marinade and place them, skin side up, on a foil-lined cookie sheet. Bake for 50 minutes to 1 hour in a 375-degree oven. Brush the chicken with the oyster sauce and sprinkle it with kumquat slivers as directed above.

▚▚

Smoked Turkey Breast with Sweet and Crunchy Cranberry Chutney

SERVES 6 TO 8

1   turkey breast (with skin, without bone), about 3½ pounds
1   recipe Marinade for Lean Birds (see page 21)
4   chunks mesquite, about 4 by 2½ inches each, soaked in water
     for 1 hour before use
     Sweet and Crunchy Cranberry Chutney (recipe follows)

1. Wash and dry the turkey breast, removing all visible fat. Place it in a large ziplock plastic bag and pour the marinade into the bag. Seal the bag and turn several times to coat the breast. Place the bag in a large bowl and marinate for 3 to 4 hours in the refrigerator, turning the bag several times.

2. Fill the smoker's charcoal pan ¾ full with briquets. Light the coals. When the briquets are partly ashen—about 20 minutes—drain the mesquite chunks and add them to the charcoal. Fill the water pan with boiling water.

3. Place the turkey breast on an ungreased grid and cover the smoker. Smoke for 1½ to 2 hours, checking the water pan and coals every 30 to 45 minutes to see if either needs to be replenished. Test for doneness by inserting a fork into the breast. If the juices run clear, it is done. If they run pink, continue smoking.

4. Remove the breast from the smoker and let sit at room temperature until somewhat cooler to touch, then pull skin from meat and discard. Serve warm or cold with Sweet and Crunchy Cranberry Chutney.

TO COOK INDOORS: Combine 1 cup water and ½ cup natural liquid smoke. Place the turkey breast in a large ziplock plastic bag and pour in the liquid smoke marinade. Seal the bag and turn several times to coat the breast. Place the bag in a large bowl and marinate in the refrigerator for 1 hour, turning the bag several times.

Remove the breast from the marinade and rub the turkey breast with 2 tablespoons unsalted butter. Sprinkle the breast with a little freshly ground pepper and garlic powder. Place the turkey on an oiled rack in a roasting pan and cover it loosely with foil. Roast in a 325-degree oven for 20 minutes, then remove the foil. Continue roasting, uncovered, for an additional 50 minutes (a total of 70 minutes—20 minutes per pound). Remove it from the oven and let sit for 15 minutes or longer before slicing. Serve as directed above.

Sweet and Crunchy Cranberry Chutney

MAKES 2¾ CUPS

1   **medium-sized tomato**
2   **cups fresh cranberries**
¾   **cup water**
1   **small onion, minced**
½   **cup raisins**
¼   **teaspoon salt**
½   **cup cider vinegar**
¼   **teaspoon freshly ground black pepper**
1   **cup firmly packed dark brown sugar**
1   **tablespoon chopped candied ginger**
½   **teaspoon ground ginger**
½   **teaspoon ground cloves**

1. Slide the tomato into boiling water to cover for 1 minute or until the skin begins to loosen. Place it under cold tap water and peel when cool. Seed and chop it coarsely.

2. In a medium-sized saucepan, combine the tomato, cranberries, water, onion, raisins and salt. Bring to a boil, reduce the heat and simmer for 8 to 10 minutes or until the cranberries pop.

3. Add the vinegar, pepper, brown sugar, candied and ground ginger and cloves. Bring to a boil, cover and simmer for 30 to 35 minutes or until thickened, stirring occasionally. Cool and spoon into a serving bowl. Serve warm, chilled or at room temperature.

Smoked Turkey with Winter Fruit Relish

SERVES 8

1 turkey, 12 pounds or less
1 medium onion, quartered
1 large carrot, cut into chunks
4 cups hickory chips or 4 large chunks hickory (4 by 2½ inches), soaked in water for 30 minutes before use
   Winter Fruit Relish (recipe follows)

1. Fill the smoker's charcoal pan ¾ full with briquets. Light the coals. Wash and dry the turkey, removing all visible fat. Place the onion quarters and carrot chunks in the turkey cavity.

2. When the coals are partly ashen, drain the hickory and place it on the coals. Fill the water pan with boiling water and place the turkey on an ungreased grid. Cover the smoker.

3. Smoke the turkey for approximately 6½ hours (the time may vary considerably depending on the temperature of the smoker), checking every 30 to 45 minutes to see if the water pan needs to be refilled and if extra briquets are needed. The turkey is done when the joints move freely and the juices run clear when the thigh is pricked with a fork. If the juices run pink, the turkey is not done.

4. Transfer the turkey to a large serving platter and let sit at room temperature for 20 to 30 minutes before carving. Discard the skin, which gets very tough during smoking, and serve the turkey, carved into slices, with Winter Fruit Relish.

TO COOK INDOORS: Place the turkey, breast side up, on an oiled rack in a deep roasting pan. Brush liberally with 3 tablespoons unsalted butter and sprinkle with freshly ground pepper and garlic powder (to give missing flavor when bird isn't smoked). Cover the breast loosely with aluminum foil. Roast, uncovered, in a 325-degree oven for 2 hours, then remove the foil. Continue roasting for an additional 2½ to 3 hours, a total of 4 to 4½ hours (approximately 20 minutes per pound). Baste the turkey with the pan juices liberally every 20 to 30

French gourmet Jean Anthelme Brillat-Savarin was grateful for the New World's gift of turkey to Europe. When confronted by the gossip that the turkey was known to the Romans or was served at Charlemagne's wedding, he offered a charming, if illogical, argument to prove this could not be true: "The face of the turkey is clearly that of a foreigner," he insisted. "No wise man could be mistaken about it."

He was correct. Turkeys were brought to Europe by the conquistadores, who appropriated them from the Aztecs, along with chocolate. Turkey was first eaten in France at the marriage of Charles IX in 1571.

minutes. Transfer it to a serving platter and let it sit at room temperature for 20 to 30 minutes before carving. Serve it sliced with Winter Fruit Relish.

Winter Fruit Relish

MAKES 3/3/4 CUPS

1   **medium-sized navel orange**
1   **medium-sized lemon**
1   **10-ounce jar kumquats**
4   **cups fresh cranberries**
2   **cups sugar**
½   **cup cranberry liqueur (or substitute orange liqueur)**

1. Using a vegetable peeler, peel the zest from half of the navel orange. Do the same with half of the lemon. Place the orange and lemon zests in a food processor fitted with the steel blade.

2. Take 4 kumquats from the jar and cut them in half. Add them to the food processor along with the cranberries and pulse until finely chopped. Transfer the mixture to a medium-sized bowl.

3. Stir in the sugar and liqueur and let stand for 45 minutes at room temperature, stirring occasionally. Spoon into a serving dish, cover and refrigerate. Serve chilled with Smoked Turkey. Garnish with the remaining kumquats if desired.

Chinese Tea-Smoked Chicken

SERVES 6

In this easy, unusual recipe, brown sugar and Chinese black tea are placed on a sheet of aluminum foil, which is then set directly on the coals. As the mixture burns, it emits an intense and aromatic smoke that flavors the chicken deliciously. If Chinese black tea and sesame oil are not available in your area, see page 182 for our list of mail-order sources.

1   cup brown sugar

½   cup loose Chinese black tea

2   chickens, about 2½ pounds each

¼   cup Oriental sesame oil

4   cups cooked large, flat, egg noodles, set in a colander to drain

2   tablespoons unsalted butter

1. Fill the smoker's charcoal pan ¾ full with briquets. Light the coals. When the briquets are ashen, fold a 2-foot sheet of aluminum foil in half. Sprinkle the brown sugar and tea over the center of the foil. Place the foil directly onto ashen coals. Fill the water pan with boiling water.

2. Wash and dry the chickens, removing all visible fat. Cut them in half lengthwise. Place the chicken halves, breast side up, on an oiled grid and cover the smoker. Smoke the chicken for 1 hour, lifting the cover after 30 minutes to see if more water or coals are needed. The chicken is done if the juices run clear when the meat is pricked with a fork.

3. Fill a medium-sized saucepan with water and bring to a boil. Remove the chickens from the smoker and transfer them to a chopping board. Brush them with the sesame oil. Cut each chicken half into 6 pieces with poultry shears or a Chinese cleaver. Remove the wings and legs, then cut each half into 4 pieces of equal width.

4. Pour the boiling water over the noodles in the colander. Shake to remove excess water and toss the noodles with the butter on a serving platter with raised sides. Quickly arrange the noodles in a flat

bed and place the chicken pieces on top of the noodles. Serve immediately.

TO COOK INDOORS: Do not try this unless you have excellent ventilation, as the room will get very smoky. Steam the chicken for 30 minutes on a rack over simmering water in a covered pot (the chicken should not touch the water). Allow to cool.

Line a wok with a double thickness of foil and sprinkle ½ cup brown sugar and ¼ cup Chinese tea over the foil. Place the chicken on a rack above the foil and cover the wok.

Place the wok over high heat for 5 minutes, then turn off the heat. Let the chicken cool in the covered wok. Do not open. When cool, brush the chicken lightly with sesame oil and cut as above. Serve at room temperature.

Smoked Long Island Duck, Peking Style

SERVES 6

The smoked duck in this recipe is not a version of Peking duck; it's merely smoked duck eaten Peking style, which means rolled in a Chinese pancake with onion and hoisin sauce—a sweet, thick, pungent sauce made from soybeans, flour, vegetables and chilies.

This recipe is as much fun to prepare as it is to eat. Before the duck goes into the smoker, it is poached for six minutes, then hung with string by its wings from the shower head to allow the fat to drip off into a pan below. Any unexpected afternoon visitor is guaranteed to run out of the guest bathroom in alarm.

We suggest serving hot steamed rice with this dish. If you want to stay in the ethnic mode, add an egg drop soup or stir-fried snow peas. You might also want to buy a jar of candied ginger in syrup, chop it coarsely and ladle it over vanilla ice cream for dessert.

Candied ginger with syrup, hoisin sauce and Oriental sesame oil are all available at Chinese or Oriental specialty shops; or see page 182 for our list of mail order sources. Since Chinese pancakes cannot be ordered by mail, if you do not live near a Chinese food store that makes them, substitute flour tortillas.

2   Long Island ducks, about 5 pounds each

4   tablespoons honey

4   tablespoons cider vinegar

1/2   teaspoon ground ginger

4   large chunks mesquite, about 4 by 2½ inches each, soaked in water for 2 hour before use

4   cinnamon sticks

SAUCE

1½ cups hoisin sauce

1   tablespoon Oriental sesame oil

2   teaspoons sugar

12   scallions

12   Chinese pancakes (or substitute flour tortillas)

1. Wash and dry the ducks. Half fill a large soup kettle with water. Bring it to a boil, reduce the heat to a simmer and add the honey, vinegar and ginger.

2. Lower 1 duck into the simmering water, breast side down, and simmer for 3 minutes. Turn the duck breast side up and simmer for another 3 minutes. Carefully lift the duck from the water and place it on a platter to drain. Repeat with the second duck.

3. Cut a 3-foot piece of string and tie 1 end around the duck wing close to the body. Tie the other end of string around the other wing. Hang the duck over the shower nozzle with a dripping pan underneath. Repeat with the other duck (you can use a longer string or hang it from a faucet). Let the ducks hang for 1 hour, then take them down and dry them with kitchen towels.

4. Cut the ducks in half lengthwise. Remove the wings and store them in a plastic bag in the freezer for another use. Fill the smoker's charcoal pan ¾ full with briquets. Light the coals. When the briquets are partly ashen, drain the mesquite and place it over the coals.

5. Fill the water pan with boiling water and add the cinnamon sticks to the pan. Arrange the dried duck halves on an ungreased grid and cover the smoker. Smoke for 1 hour and 45 minutes, checking every 45 minutes to see if additional water or charcoal is needed. The duck is done if the juices run clear when the meat is pricked with a fork.

6. While the duck is smoking, prepare the sauce: Place the hoisin, sesame oil and sugar in a small saucepan. Bring to a boil over medium heat, stirring to combine. Remove from the heat and pour the sauce into a bowl. Let sit at room temperature. If made more than 2 hours in advance, store in the refrigerator.

7. Cut the green parts off the scallions, leaving 12 white onion sticks. Place 1 on a cutting board and make several 1/2-inch-long parallel cuts on the end as if you were making a broom. Repeat on the other side of the scallion. Repeat this process with the remaining 11 scallions. Store them in the refrigerator in a plastic bag until ready to use.

8. Remove the duck halves from the smoker and remove their skin. Let cool a few moments. Just before serving time, stack the pancakes in the center of a large piece of foil. Wrap the foil around the pancakes, twisting it at the top, and place them in a 350-degree oven for 10 minutes.

9. Cut the meat into bite-sized pieces, then arrange the meat on a platter along with the scallion brooms, pancakes and hoisin sauce. To assemble: Ladle a thin line of hoisin sauce down the center of a pancake. Arrange a thin strip of duck on top of the sauce. Place the scallion broom over the duck. Roll the pancake to eat.

TO COOK INDOORS: Poach and hang the ducks as directed. Cut the ducks in half, but do not remove the wings as the duck will not be smoked. Place the duck halves, skin side up, on a rack set in a high-sided, foil-lined roasting pan. Add 1/2 inch water to the pan. Roast for 45 minutes to 1 hour at 425 degrees. Reduce the heat to 375 degrees, turn the duck halves over and roast for another 45 minutes, uncovered. There is no need to peel the skin off as the duck is not smoked.

Let the ducks cool a few moments, then cut off the wings and arrange them on a platter. Remove the skin and meat, cut it into bite-sized pieces and put it on the platter with the wings. Serve with the hoisin sauce, scallion brooms and pancakes.

PEKING DUCK: Peking duck, one of the most famous Chinese dishes, is really a three-course meal. It begins with a serving of crisp, brown, almost brittle duck skin rolled in delicate pancakes topped with a tiny scallion and sweet, spicy hoisin sauce.

This is followed by some soft, flavorful duck meat tossed with crisp bean sprouts and hot peppers. The final course is a rich broth made from the carcass and simmered for hours to extract the flavor.

To get the skin so extraordinarily crisp, the chef works for hours. First he massages the skin to loosen it, then he blows through a tiny hole in the skin, causing the duck to puff like a balloon. (In America, chefs use bicycle pumps.)

Next, he rubs it with a honey, spice and vinegar marinade, then hangs it outside in a cold Peking wind. (In America, chefs put the duck in front of a blowing fan.) Finally, the duck is roasted in a vertical wood-burning oven, which is how the skin achieves its final degree of crispness.

Chinese gourmets insist that the real Peking duck cannot be made outside China because no one knows the proper procedure and because the vertical oven is not available. This may be true—Chinese chefs study for a year in China before they feel confident to attempt it.

Smoked Long Island Duck with Apple and Crème Fraîche Sauce

SERVES 4 TO 6

2	Long Island ducks, about 5 pounds each
$1/2$	cup honey
$1/4$	cup cider vinegar
$1/2$	teaspoon ground ginger
$1/2$	cup crab-apple jelly
2	tablespoons water
4	large chunks mesquite, each about $2^{1/2}$ by 4 inches long, soaked in water for 1 hour before use

4   cinnamon sticks
3   large apples, cored
½   cup water
1   teaspoon ground cinnamon
3   teaspoons sugar
1½   cups crème fraîche
½   teaspoon (heaping) freshly grated nutmeg

1. Wash and dry the ducks. Half fill a large soup kettle with water. Bring it to a boil, reduce the heat to a simmer and add the honey, vinegar and ginger.

2. Lower 1 duck into the simmering water, breast side down, and simmer for 3 minutes. Turn the duck breast side up and simmer for another 3 minutes. Carefully lift the duck from the water and place it on a platter to drain. Repeat with the other duck.

3. Cut a 3-foot piece of string and tie 1 end around the duck wing close to the body. Tie the other end of the string around the other wing. Hang the duck over the shower nozzle with a dripping pan underneath. Repeat with the other duck, hanging it from a different faucet (or on a longer string) with a dripping pan underneath. Let the ducks hang for 1 hour, then take them down and dry with kitchen towels.

4. Put the crab-apple jelly in a saucepan with the 2 tablespoons water and simmer over medium heat, watching constantly, for 5 minutes or until dissolved. Cut the ducks in half. Remove the wings and store them in a plastic bag in the freezer for another use. Brush the duck halves completely with the melted jelly.

5. Fill the smoker's charcoal pan ¾ full with briquets. Light the coals. When the coals are partly ashen, drain the mesquite and place it on top of the coals. Fill the water pan with boiling water and add the cinnamon sticks to the pan. Place the ducks, skin side up, on an ungreased grid and cover the smoker. Smoke for 1 hour and 45 minutes, checking every 45 minutes to see if more water or charcoal is needed. The ducks are done if the juices run clear when the meat is pricked with a fork.

6. Place the apples and ½ cup water in a baking dish with raised sides. Mix together the cinnamon and sugar and spoon 1 teaspoon of the

mixture into each apple cavity. Bake for 1 hour at 375 degrees. Remove the skin from the apples and mash the flesh in a bowl. Add 3 tablespoons drippings from the pan bottom, along with the crème fraîche and nutmeg.

7. Transfer the ducks to a serving platter and remove their skin. Bring the ducks to the table and serve with the warm apple–crème fraîche sauce.

TO COOK INDOORS: Poach and hang the ducks as directed. Cut the ducks in half, but do not remove the wings as the duck will not be smoked. Place the duck halves, skin side up, on a rack set in a high-sided, foil-lined roasting pan. Add ½ inch water to the pan. Roast for 45 minutes to 1 hour at 425 degrees. Reduce the heat to 375 degrees, turn the halves and roast for another 45 minutes, uncovered. There is no need to remove the skins as the duck is not smoked.

Let the ducks cool a few moments, then cut them into 12 pieces: Using poultry shears or a Chinese cleaver, cut off the wings and legs and place them on a platter. Cut each duck half into 4 equal pieces, as directed. Arrange the 24 duck pieces on a serving platter and serve with the hot apple–crème fraîche sauce.

Smoked Turkey Breast with Pecan Butter

SERVES 4

The whole turkey breast with the skin called for in this recipe is available in supermarkets.

1   turkey breast with skin without bone, about 3½ pounds

PECAN BUTTER

½   cup (1 stick) unsalted butter, at room temperature

½   cup ground pecans

**4   chunks mesquite, each about 4 by 2½ inches, soaked in water
for 1 hour before use**

1. Fill the smoker's charcoal pan ¾ full with briquets. Light the coals. Wash and dry the turkey breast, removing any visible fat. Carefully insert your finger between the skin and the flesh on top of the breast to make a pocket. Be careful not to tear the skin. Work deeper and deeper, enlarging the pocket slowly. Do not loosen the skin on the sides of the breast.

2. Prepare the Pecan Butter: Mix the butter and pecans together in a small bowl. Using your fingers, spread the mixture under the turkey skin, covering the top of the breast evenly.

3. When the coals are partly ashen, drain the mesquite and place it on the coals. Fill the water pan with boiling water. Place the turkey breast on an ungreased grid, skin side up, and cover the smoker.

4. Smoke the turkey for 2 hours, checking every 30 to 45 minutes to see if additional water or coals are needed. To check for doneness, insert a fork into the breast. If the juices run clear, the turkey is done; if they run pink, the turkey needs additional smoking.

5. Transfer the turkey to a cutting board and let sit for 20 to 30 minutes. Carefully remove and discard the skin without disturbing the pecans. Carve the turkey and serve warm or cold.

TO COOK INDOORS: Rub the turkey skin with 2 to 3 tablespoons olive oil, then sprinkle lightly with salt, freshly ground pepper and garlic powder for flavor. Spread with pecan butter as in step 2 above. Place it on an oiled rack in a deep-sided pan and cover it loosely with aluminum foil. Roast for 20 minutes in a 325-degree oven, then remove the foil. Continue roasting for an additional hour (1 hour and 20 minutes altogether) or until done. Check for doneness as above and let sit as directed before carving.

Feasts from the Grill

What is more fun than a feast? This section includes whole menu feasts for several occasions, ranging from a Christmas goose and Thanksgiving turkey feast to a caveman feast for kids with hand-held grilled turkey legs, corn on the cob, watermelon and cookies.

Caveman Party

This is a great party for children. They can dress in torn clothing (cut old T-shirts to resemble the over-one-shoulder skins that comic-book cavemen wear), take their shoes off and eat a whole meal without knives or forks. Bring the food to the table on platters without silverware, but do include a stack of napkins and some wet naps if possible. And don't forget a bowl for the watermelon seeds. If the children are young, you can rent videotapes of old Flintstones cartoons.

These recipes are intended for six children, but they can be doubled easily.

MENU
Barbecued Turkey Drumsticks
Corn Grilled in Husks with Honey Butter
Grill-Cooked Small Red Potatoes in Foil
Giant Dinosaur Cookies
Watermelon Slices
Caveman Juice (Lemonade)

Barbecued Turkey Drumsticks

SERVES 6

BARBECUE SAUCE
3 tablespoons vegetable oil
¾ cup minced scallions
2 cloves garlic, minced
1½ cups bottled chili sauce
¼ cup cider vinegar
¼ cup brown sugar
3 tablespoons tomato paste
2 teaspoons Worcestershire sauce

¼ teaspoon salt

¼ teaspoon freshly ground black pepper

6   turkey drumsticks, as small as possible

12 small red potatoes

½ cup (1 stick) unsalted butter, at room temperature

3   tablespoons honey

½ teaspoon fresh lemon juice

6   ears of corn, unhusked

1. Prepare the Barbecue Sauce: Heat the oil in a saucepan over medium heat. Sauté the scallions and garlic for about 5 minutes, stirring occasionally, until softened. Add the chili sauce, vinegar, sugar, tomato paste, Worcestershire sauce, salt and pepper. Simmer for 5 minutes longer. Transfer to a serving bowl and allow to cool.

2. Wash and dry the turkey legs. Place them in a glass or ceramic dish and brush them with sauce on all sides. Cover the dish with plastic wrap and let it sit at room temperature for 1 hour (or 2 hours in the refrigerator), turning occasionally. Transfer the remaining sauce to a sauceboat.

3. Prepare the grill for the Direct Grilling Method (see page 16). Light the coals. When the briquets become ashen, place the legs on a lightly oiled grid over the ashen coals. Grill, over direct heat for 40 to 50 minutes, checking or turning the legs every 5 minutes and brushing with the sauce each time.

4. Wash the potatoes, but do not peel them. Tear off 6 small aluminum foil squares and wrap 2 potatoes in each. When the turkey legs have been on the grill for 10 minutes, place the potato packets on the edges of the grill for 30 minutes.

5. While the legs and potatoes are grilling, combine the butter, honey and lemon juice in a small bowl. Pull back the corn husks and remove the silk. Spread each ear with the honey-butter mixture. Bring the husks back up around the corn to protect it on the grill. When the turkey legs have been on the grill for 30 minutes, set the corn on the grill for about 10 minutes. Turn the corn once after 5 minutes.

6. When the legs are done, transfer them to a serving platter. Arrange the corn in its husks on a second platter with the potatoes and bring to the table with the sauceboat of Barbecue Sauce.

When the grilled food is ready, add ice to the lemonade and pass napkins with the food. For dessert, bring the cookies and watermelon to the table.

TO COOK INDOORS: Arrange the marinated turkey legs on a foil-lined cookie sheet and bake for 1 hour and 15 minutes at 375 degrees, turning once after 25 minutes and brushing with sauce. Arrange the potatoes in foil packets and put them in the oven 35 minutes after the legs have been in the oven. Fill a soup kettle ⅔ full with water and bring it to a boil. Shuck the corn and slide it into the water. Boil the corn for 4 to 10 minutes (depending on the freshness of the corn), until tender; spread the corn with honey butter before bringing it to the table.

Giant Dinosaur Cookies

MAKES 20 TO 22 COOKIES

½   cup (1 stick) unsalted butter, at room temperature
1   cup sugar
½   teaspoon salt
½   teaspoon ground cloves
½   teaspoon freshly grated nutmeg
2   teaspoons ground ginger
¼   teaspoon ground allspice
1   teaspoon baking soda
1   cup dark molasses
½   cup water
3½ cups all-purpose flour

1. In the large bowl of an electric mixer, beat the butter with the sugar, salt, cloves, nutmeg, ginger, allspice and baking soda. When light and fluffy, add molasses and beat again.

2. Add the water and flour alternately in 3 additions, beating well after each addition. Cover the dough and chill in the refrigerator for 3 hours.

3. Preheat the oven to 375 degrees. Divide the dough in half. Roll one half on a lightly floured board, using a floured rolling pin, to a thickness of between ⅛ and ¼ inch thick—very thin. Cut out 4-inch rounds with a cookie cutter and carefully transfer them to a greased cookie sheet, using a floured spatula.

4. Bake the cookies for 10 minutes at 375 degrees, watching them carefully during the last few minutes. Let them sit on the baking sheet for 3 to 5 minutes or until solid enough to transfer to a wire rack to cool.

5. Store the cookies in an airtight container at room temperature.

Thanksgiving Turkey Feast

The first Thanksgiving turkeys and waterfowl were probably grilled outdoors in a fashion similar to the one in this recipe.

MENU

Thanksgiving Grilled Turkey
Apricot Bread Stuffing
Raspberry Sauce
Sweet Potato Casserole Pie
Grilled Turnips on Sticks

Thanksgiving Grilled Turkey with Apricot Bread Stuffing

SERVES 8

1   free-range turkey, about 12 to 14 pounds, with giblets and neck reserved

"I wish the bald eagle had not been chosen as the representative of our country; he is a bird of bad moral character. . . . The turkey is a much more respectable bird, and withal a true original native of America." — Benjamin Franklin in a letter to Sarah Bache, January 1784.

RASPBERRY MARINADE

1   cup virgin olive oil

½   cup raspberry vinegar

⅛   teaspoon freshly ground black pepper

⅛   teaspoon ground ginger

⅛   teaspoon dried chervil

⅓   cup fresh or frozen raspberries, mashed

1   teaspoon ground ginger for aromatic
     Apricot Bread Stuffing (recipe follows)
     Raspberry Sauce (recipe follows)

1. Have butcher split the turkey down the backbone. Wash and dry the turkey, removing all visible fat. Open the turkey on the counter so both halves lie flat. Using a wooden mallet or rolling pin, pound the turkey breastbone down, breaking it so that the butterflied sides lie flat.

2. Prepare the Raspberry Marinade: Combine the olive oil, vinegar, pepper, ginger, chervil and raspberries in a medium-sized bowl. Place the turkey, butterfly fashion, in a large pan with raised sides. Pour the marinade over the turkey, turning it so that all sides are coated with the marinade. Place it in the refrigerator for 3 hours, basting on all sides with marinade as often as possible.

3. Remove the turkey from the marinade and place it on the counter, butterfly fashion, with the front of the turkey facing you. Take off any rings or bracelets. You will be loosening the skin from the breast meat on both sides of the breastbone. Carefully, without tearing the skin, insert your fingers between the skin and the flesh on 1 side of the breastbone to make a pocket. Work deeper and deeper, enlarging the pocket until your whole hand is inside, under the skin. Although the skin is fastened to the breastbone and fastened at the bottom of the drumstick, you'll still be able to make a large pocket at the thigh and down slightly past the top of the drumstick. Repeat this process on the other side of the breastbone.

4. Prepare the Apricot Bread Stuffing. Divide it in half. Push the stuffing deeply into both sides of the turkey, all the way down to the drumsticks, using half the stuffing for each side.

5. Prepare the grill for the Indirect Grilling Method (see page 17). Light the coals. When the briquets become ashen, add the ground ginger to the water in the dripping pan.

6. Place the turkey, butterfly fashion, on an oiled grid, skin side up, over the dripping pan. Grill, covered, over indirect heat for 2 to 2½ hours without turning. Check every 30 to 45 minutes to see if the water has evaporated or if more coals are needed. To check the turkey for doneness, insert a fork deeply into the leg and twist slightly. If the juices run clear, the turkey is done. If they are pink, the turkey needs additional cooking.

7. Transfer the turkey to a large serving platter and let rest for 15 to 30 minutes before carving. Serve with a helping of Apricot Bread Stuffing, Raspberry Sauce and Sweet Potato Casserole Pie.

TO COOK INDOORS: Marinate the turkey and stuff it as directed. Place it skin side up on an oiled rack in a roasting pan, butterfly fashion. Fill the pan with ½ inch of water and sliced onion. Cover the turkey loosely with aluminum foil. Roast for 90 minutes at 325 degrees. Remove the foil and continue roasting for 2½ hours, uncovered. Transfer the turkey to a serving platter and let sit at room temperature for 15 to 30 minutes before carving. Serve as directed above.

Apricot Bread Stuffing

MAKES 7 CUPS

6	tablespoons unsalted butter
½	cup chopped celery
1	large onion, minced
1	large carrot, grated
2	cups chopped dried apricots
5	cups day-old bread cubes, made from crustless bread
¼	teaspoon dried thyme
⅛	teaspoon salt
⅛	teaspoon freshly ground black pepper
⅛	teaspoon ground cloves

1. Heat the butter in a large frying pan. Add the celery, onion and carrot and cook, uncovered, over medium heat, stirring occasionally for about 5 minutes or until the vegetables are soft. Add the apricots, bread cubes, thyme, salt, pepper and cloves. Continue cooking over medium heat until everything is well combined.

Raspberry Sauce

MAKES 1½ CUP

1   turkey neck and giblets
1   8-ounce can pitted apricots
3   shallots, minced
¾   cup dry red wine
3   tablespoons unsalted butter
1   tablespoon all-purpose flour
¼   teaspoon salt
½   teaspoon freshly ground pepper
2   cups fresh raspberries (or substitute frozen whole raspberries)

1. Rinse the turkey neck and giblets and place them in a small saucepan with water to cover. Bring to a boil, reduce the heat and simmer for 20 to 30 minutes or until the giblets are tender. Cool, dice them finely and discard the bones and cartilage. Strain the cooking liquid and reserve 1 cup of it.

2. Puree the apricots in a food processor fitted with the steel blade or a blender. Reserve. Place the shallots in a small saucepan with the wine and simmer for 10 minutes over medium heat. Strain the mixture, discarding the shallots, and return the wine to the saucepan. Heat the butter in another saucepan. Add the flour and cook over medium heat, stirring constantly with a wire whisk, for about 1 minute.

3. Slowly stir in the wine, whisking constantly, and cook until slightly thickened. Whisk in the apricot puree, minced giblets and salt and pepper. Add the raspberries, heat for a few seconds and transfer the sauce to a sauceboat.

Note: If the sauce is going to sit for a while before serving, do not add the raspberries until the sauce is reheated and about to be brought to the table with the turkey.

Sweet Potato Casserole Pie

SERVES 9 TO 12

This delicious pie, made in a 9- by 12-inch casserole dish, is easily made. Its crust is made of soft cookie dough, hand-kneaded and pressed into the casserole dish rather than rolled, and it's topped with a meringue that bakes along with the pie. Serve it as a sweet potato side dish or as a dessert at Thanksgiving.

CRUST

1   cup (2 sticks) unsalted butter

2½ cups all-purpose flour

2   egg yolks (reserve the whites for the meringue)

¼   cup sour cream

½   teaspoon fresh lemon juice

FILLING

2   1-pound cans sweeet potatoes, drained

2   egg yolks (reserve the whites for the meringue)

⅔   cup sugar

¼   cup half-and-half

¼   teaspoon freshly grated nutmeg

1   tablespoon fresh lemon juice

4   tablespoons unsalted butter

MERINGUE

4   egg whites (reserved from the eggs used for the crust and filling), at room temperature

1   cup sugar

1   teaspoon vanilla extract

1. Prepare the crust: Place the butter, flour, egg yolks, sour cream and lemon juice in a food processor fitted with the steel blade. Pulse a few times until a soft ball of dough is formed. Pat the dough onto the bottom and 1 inch up the sides of a greased 9- by 12-inch casserole dish.

2. Preheat the oven to 400 degrees. Place a large sheet of aluminum foil over the crust and carefully mold it against the bottom and sides. This will help the crust keep its shape as it bakes without the filling. Set the casserole in the oven for 20 to 25 minutes at 400 degrees, until it is cooked through and just starting to brown. Remove it from the oven and carefully lift off the foil. Allow it to cool.

3. Prepare the filling: Beat together the sweet potatoes, egg yolks, sugar, half-and-half, nutmeg, lemon juice and butter in the large bowl of an electric mixer. Mix at low speed until the ingredients are completely combined and the mixture is fluffy. Spoon the mixture into the cooling crust.

4. Prepare the meringue: Beat the egg whites in the large bowl of an electric mixer until they form stiff peaks. With the mixer still running, add the sugar, $1/3$ cup at a time. When well mixed, add the vanilla.

5. Preheat the oven to 350 degrees. Spoon the meringue over the filling, sealing it to the edges to prevent shrinking. Bake the pie in the oven for 35 to 40 minutes, until the meringue has begun to color. Remove it from the oven and allow it to cool. Serve warm or at room temperature.

Grilled Turnips on a Stick

SERVES 6

If you use baby turnips in this recipe, the grilling time will be shorter. If you wish, you can also substitute tarragon, basil or parsley for the oregano. Cook the turnips directly over the hot coals immediately after taking the turkey off the grill.

12 wooden barbecue skewers, soaked in water for 30 minutes
     before use
1   teaspoon salt
12 medium turnips, peeled
     Virgin olive oil for brushing turnips
1   teaspoon dried oregano

1. Fill a soup kettle half full with water and add the salt. Bring to a boil and slide the turnips into the water. Reduce the heat and simmer for about 12 minutes or until the turnips are tender enough to pierce with a fork. Drain and cool the turnips.

2. Drain the skewers. Quarter the turnips and thread 4 quarters onto each skewer. Brush on all sides with olive oil and sprinkle with oregano.

3. Grill, covered, over direct heat for 9 minutes, turning every 3 minutes or until done to taste. Transfer to a serving platter and bring to the table. Serve 2 skewers to each guest.

TO COOK INDOORS: Place the skewered turnips on a foil-covered cookie sheet and broil 6 inches from the flame for 9 minutes, turning every 3 minutes or until done.

Grilled Mexican Feast

MENU
Quail Adovada
Blue Cornbread Madeleines
Green Salad with Tart Vinaigrette

Quail Adovada

SERVES 6

In New Mexico, the words *carne adovada* mean "pickled meat" and refer to a popular regional preparation in which poultry or meat is marinated in a mixture of coarsely ground peppers, garlic and water, then grilled over charcoal. The coarse grind of indigenous peppers—which has its own distinct flavor and piquancy—is known as *chili caribe*.

In this version, a small game bird—quail—replaces the more usual chicken and, because of its small size, spends only 10 minutes on the grill.

If chili caribe is not available in your area, see page 182 for our list of mail-order sources.

12   quail, 4 to 5 ounces each

ADOVADA MARINADE
¾   cup chili caribe
4   cloves garlic, peeled
1   teaspoon white vinegar
1   teaspoon sugar
1   cup water

1. Wash and dry the quail. Using sharp kitchen scissors, butterfly the

quail by cutting each through the breastbone. Open and flatten the quail.

2. Place the chili caribe, garlic cloves, white vinegar, sugar and water in a food processor fitted with the steel blade and pulse until coarsely pureed.

3. Divide the quail between 2 large ziplock plastic bags and pour half of the marinade into each bag. Seal the bags and turn each a few times to coat the quail. Place the bags on cookie sheets and marinate at room temperature for 1 hour (or 2 hours in the refrigerator), turning occasionally.

4. Prepare the grill for the Direct Grilling Method (see page 16). Light the coals. When the briquets become ashen, remove the quail from the marinade (do not wipe off the excess marinade). Reserve the marinade. Place each quail, skin side down, on an oiled grid over the ashen coals. Cook, covered, over direct heat for 10 minutes, turning the quail after 5 minutes and brushing with the marinade.

5. Transfer the quail to a serving platter and bring to the table with warm Blue Cornbread Madeleines.

TO COOK INDOORS: Broil the marinated quail 6 inches from the heat for 10 minutes. Broil, skin side up, for 5 minutes, then turn and broil, skin side down, for 5 minutes longer. Serve as directed.

Blue Cornbread Madeleines

MAKES 24

Blue cornbread, another New Mexico specialty, is made from the blue corn that grows in the Southwest. Blue corn has a bland taste. But the cornbread it makes has a much more subtle flavor and a finer texture than that made with yellow corn.

Blue cornbread is usually baked in a cast-iron skillet. This version uses a French madeleine pan, which has small narrow indentations and is similar to corn stick pans, except that the molds are fluted on the bottom like seashells. When made in this cunning shape, blue cornbread seems to taste even more delicate than the original.
If you have only one madeleine mold, bake this recipe in two batches,

greasing the pan after each batch. If blue cornmeal and madeleine pans are not available in your area, see page 182 for our list of mail-order sources.

Vegetable shortening for greasing pan
3   **tablespoons unsalted butter**
1   **cup blue cornmeal**
¾   **cup all-purpose flour**
½   **teaspoon salt**
½   **teaspoon baking soda**
2   **teaspoons baking powder**
1   **large egg**
1¼ **cups buttermilk**

1. Grease 2 madeleine pans (12 molds each) with vegetable shortening and set aside.

2. Using the large bowl of an electric mixer or a food processor fitted with the steel blade, combine the butter, blue cornmeal, flour, salt, baking soda, baking powder, egg and buttermilk. Mix until well combined.

3. Preheat the oven to 425 degrees. Spoon the batter into each madeleine indentation, filling it to just below the rim. Bake in the oven for 10 to 12 minutes at 425 degrees or until the madeleines begin pulling away from the sides and are firm to the touch.

4. Let sit in the molds at room temperature for 5 minutes. Turn the madeleines out and arrange them on a serving platter. Bring to the table immediately while warm. Madeleines are delicious plain, or you can serve them with butter.

Green Salad with Tart Vinaigrette

SERVES 8

4   cups washed and drained Boston lettuce, torn into bite-sized pieces

4   cups washed and drained Romaine lettuce, torn into bite-sized pieces

1   medium red onion, peeled, cut into paper-thin slices

2   tablespoons fresh lemon juice

2   ripe avocados, peeled, cut into ¾-inch chunks

Tart Vinaigrette

4   tablespoons fresh lemon juice

2   teaspoons Dijon mustard

1   clove garlic, minced

¼   teaspoon salt

⅛   teaspoon freshly ground black pepper

½   cup virgin olive oil

¼   cup safflower oil

1. Toss Boston and Romaine lettuce together in a large salad bowl. Add onion slices.

2. Sprinkle lemon juice on avocado chunks and add to the salad bowl. Set aside.

3. Prepare the dressing: Place lemon juice in a small bowl and wisk in mustard, garlic, salt, and pepper. Continue to wisk as you add the olive oil and then the safflower oil in a steady stream.

4. Pour dressing over salad and toss until the leaves are well coated.

Grilled Korean Feast

Korean Lettuce Sandwiches

SERVES 6

Some Korean restaurants in this country feature grills set in the center of each table for patrons to grill their own food, as they do in Korea. Waitresses bring platters of marinated chicken cut into strips, along with mushrooms, onions and whole garlic cloves, all of which are arranged on the hot grid and cooked by everyone at the table.

Patrons then make lettuce sandwiches by placing 1 or 2 grilled chicken strips on a lettuce leaf, topping this with some grilled onions, grilled mushrooms and a little hot red bean paste sauce. The whole thing is then rolled up and eaten. Some people even add some of the marinated salads, served as side dishes, to the sandwich rather than eating them as side dishes. Spicy food lovers may want to buy a jar of Korean kim chee—a peppery cabbage pickle—to add to their sandwiches as well.

This recipe uses an exotic ingredient called *kochu chang*, a hot red bean paste made from pureed soybeans and rice, then mixed with red pepper to give it a spicy kick. This dark red puree has a mild, pleasant odor and is so good you may want to eat it as is right out of the container. Be careful not to confuse it with the sweet red bean paste sold in Japanese markets.

Hot red bean paste, kim chee, Oriental sesame oil and Japanese light soy sauce are all available in Korean markets or Oriental food stores; or see page 182 for our list of mail-order sources.

Three Korean Salads (recipe follows)

MARINADE
3   scallions, cut into 1-inch pieces
6   large cloves garlic, peeled and halved

½   cup Japanese soy sauce

6   tablespoons water

½   cup Oriental sesame oil

¼   cup sugar

3   large chicken breasts, 10–12 ounces each, skinned, boned and halved

HOT RED BEAN PASTE SAUCE

1   cup hot red bean paste (kochu chang)

4   tablespoons water

2   tablespoons plus 2 teaspoons sugar

2   tablespoons plus 2 teaspoons Japanese soy sauce

2   tablespoons Oriental sesame oil

24 large lettuce leaves, such as red or green leaf lettuce or Romaine, rinsed well

3   large onions, cut into ¼-inch slices

48 mushrooms, halved and threaded onto metal or wooden skewers (soak wooden skewers in water for 30 minutes before use)

1. Prepare the Three Korean Salads. Arrange each in a bowl, cover and refrigerate.

2. Prepare the marinade: Combine the scallions, garlic, soy sauce, water, sesame oil and sugar in a food processor fitted with the steel blade and pulse until the ingredients are finely chopped but not pureed.

3. Wash and dry the chicken breast halves. Place them in a large zip-lock plastic bag. Add the marinade. Seal the bag and turn it several times to coat the breasts. Place the bag on a cookie sheet and marinate at room temperature for 1 hour (or 2 hours in the refrigerator), turning occasionally.

4. Prepare the Hot Red Bean Paste Sauce: Combine the hot red bean paste, water, sugar, soy sauce and sesame oil in a serving bowl. Mix well.

5. Place the individual lettuce leaves on a platter and bring them to the table with the vegetable salads and Hot Red Bean Paste Sauce.

6. Prepare the grill for the Direct Grilling Method (see page 16). Light

the coals. When the briquets become ashen, lay the onion slices and skewered mushrooms on an oiled grid over the ashen coals and cook, uncovered, over direct heat for 10 minutes or until lightly charred. Turn once every 5 minutes. Push the onions and mushrooms to the outermost edges of the grill to keep them warm.

7. Remove the breasts from the marinade, reserving the marinade. Place the breasts on an oiled grid over direct heat. Grill, covered, for 10 minutes, turning after 5 minutes and brushing with the reserved marinade.

8. Transfer the chicken and vegetables to a serving platter and bring to the table. Each guest should cut his own chicken into strips before making the lettuce sandwiches.

TO COOK INDOORS: Place the marinated breast halves on a foil-covered cookie sheet and broil 6 inches from the flame for 7 minutes, turning after 2 minutes, and adding mushrooms and onions. Watch carefully. Serve as directed above.

Three Korean Salads

SERVES 6

1   pound bean sprouts
1   pound fresh spinach
1   pound small cucumbers
1   tablespoon sesame seeds
1   large red bell pepper, cut into fine julienne strips (or substitute green bell pepper)
2   scallions, green part only, finely chopped
1   clove garlic, very finely minced

BEAN SPROUT AND SPINACH SALAD DRESSING
8   teaspoons Japanese soy sauce
4   teaspoons Oriental sesame oil
1   tablespoon Japanese rice vinegar
½   teaspoon sugar
⅛   teaspoon cayenne pepper, or to taste

CUCUMBER SALAD DRESSING

4   teaspoons rice vinegar

2   teaspoons Oriental sesame oil

¼   teaspoon salt

¼   teaspoon sugar

⅛   teaspoon cayenne pepper

1. Fill a soup kettle half full with water and bring to a boil. Drop the bean sprouts into the water and cook for 1 minute. Remove and place them under cold running water. Shake well, dry with kitchen towels and place in a bowl. Repeat with the spinach, squeezing gently but thoroughly with kitchen towels to get it as dry as possible. Chop the spinach coarsely, then place it in a second bowl.

2. Peel the cucumbers. Cut them in half lengthwise and remove the seeds. Cut them into thin slices and place them in a kitchen towel (do not use paper towels). Squeeze gently several times to remove excess water. Place the cucumbers in a third bowl.

3. Toast the sesame seeds: Place them in a single layer in a medium-sized frying pan and set over medium heat. Cook for 1 minute, then stir with a wooden spoon for a few more moments until the seeds begin to brown. When they are lightly toasted, remove them from the heat and immediately pour them into a cool dish. Reserve for sprinkling on salads.

4. Sprinkle half the red bell pepper strips over the bean sprouts and half over the cucumbers. Sprinkle half the scallions over the bean sprouts and half over the cucumbers. Sprinkle the minced garlic over the spinach.

5. Prepare the Bean Sprout and Spinach Salad Dressing: Combine all the dressing ingredients in a small bowl. Taste for sweetness, adding a little additional sugar if desired. Mix well and divide the mixture between the bean sprouts and spinach, tossing each well with the dressing.

6. Prepare the Cucumber Salad Dressing: Combine all dressing ingredients in a small bowl. Mix well, then sprinkle over the cucumbers and toss well.

7. Cover the salads well with plastic wrap or place them, separately, in closed plastic bags and chill in the refrigerator until serving time. Sprinkle each salad with 1 teaspoon toasted sesame seeds before bringing it to the table.

Grilled Christmas Goose Feast

MENU
Grilled Christmas Goose
Sauce for the Goose
Real Mashed Potatoes
Broccoli on the Grill
Mock Mince Pie

Grilled Christmas Goose

SERVES 4 TO 6

The hickory chips in this recipe are purposefully not soaked in water so that they will create dry heat.

1	**domestic goose, about 10 pounds**
1/4	**teaspoon black freshly ground pepper**
4	**whole cloves**
1	**medium yellow onion, cut into quarters**
1	**tablespoon olive oil**
1/4	**teaspoon ground dried sage**
2/3	**cup hickory chips**
1	**navel orange, with skin, cut into thin slices for garnish**

1. Prepare the grill for the Indirect Grilling Method (see page 17). Light the coals. Wash and dry the goose, removing any visible fat. Use poultry shears to remove the wing tips and second joints of the wings, reserving them for another use. Prick the goose all over its body with a fork.

2. Sprinkle the goose cavity with the pepper. Insert 1 whole clove into each onion quarter and place the onion quarters in the goose cavity.

Brush the outside of the goose lightly with olive oil. Use your fingers to rub the sage onto the breast and legs.

3. When the coals are ashen, toss 1/3 cup of the dry hickory chips onto each bank of coals. Place the goose on an ungreased grid, breast side up, over the dripping pan. Cover the grill and open the dampers in both the cover and the kettle bottom. Grill, covered, over indirect heat for 3 hours, checking every 30 to 45 minutes to see if more water or coals are needed.

4. Test the goose for doneness by inserting a fork into the thickest part of the leg. If the juices run clear, the goose is done. If they run pink, the goose needs additional grilling time. Remove the goose from the grill and place it on a cutting board. Let stand 20 to 30 minutes before carving.

5. To carve: Disjoint the drumsticks and wings and arrange them on a serving platter. Cut the breast and thighs into slices and arrange them on the platter. Garnish the platter with the orange slices. Bring to the table with a sauceboat of hot gravy and a bowl of hot mashed potatoes.

TO COOK INDOORS: Prepare the goose as directed. Place it on a rack in a roasting pan, breast side down, and press a sheet of foil over the goose. Place the goose in a 400-degree oven for 1 hour, pouring off the grease that collects in the bottom of the pan every 30 minutes. Lower the heat to 350 degrees, turn the breast side up with oven mitts and discard the foil. Roast the goose, uncovered, breast side up, for a second hour, pouring off the grease every 30 minutes. After 2 hours, remove the goose from the oven and prick it all over with a fork. Return the goose to the oven and roast it for 1 more hour (making a total of 3 hours). Continue roasting until the goose is golden brown all over with crispy skin. The leg joints should move freely and the juices should run clear when the meat is pricked with a fork. Transfer the goose to a cutting board and let sit for 30 minutes before carving. Transfer to a serving platter and carve at the table.

▲▲▲▼▼▼

Sauce for the Goose

MAKES 3 CUPS

Although some recipes may use goose fat in place of the butter, the taste is very heavy and fatty and we don't recommend it.

- 1/3   **cup unsalted butter**
- 1/3   **cup all-purpose flour**
- 1   **quart chicken broth, heated**
- 1/2   **cup dry white wine plus additional wine for thinning sauce when ready to serve**
- 1/4   **teaspoon salt**
- 1/4   **teaspoon freshly ground black pepper**
- 1/4   **teaspoon dried thyme**
- 1/4   **teaspoon dried sage**
- 1   **tablespoon chopped fresh parsley**

1. Heat the butter in a heavy-bottomed saucepan. Add the flour, stirring constantly with a wire whisk. Cook over low heat, stirring constantly, for about 10 minutes.

2. Add the broth, a little at a time, stirring constantly after each addition. Add the wine, stir well, then add the salt, pepper, thyme and sage and simmer for 20 minutes longer over low heat, stirring often with a wire whisk.

3. Allow to cool, then store, covered, in the refrigerator. Reheat at serving time, adding a little additional broth or white wine if necessary to thin it, stirring well with a wire whisk. Transfer the gravy to a serving bowl and sprinkle it with the parsley. Serve immediately.

Real Mashed Potatoes

SERVES 6

6   large Idaho potatoes, peeled and quartered
    Pinch salt
2   tablespoons unsalted butter
6   tablespoons half-and-half
$\frac{1}{4}$ teaspoon salt
$\frac{1}{4}$ teaspoon freshly ground white pepper

1. Place the potatoes in a large saucepan and add water to cover with a pinch of salt. Bring to a boil, reduce the heat and simmer for about 20 minutes or until the potatoes can be pierced easily with a fork.

2. Drain the potatoes and transfer them to a large nonstick frying pan. Cook the potato quarters over medium heat for 4 minutes, shaking and stirring often with a wooden spoon to dry the potatoes.

3. Transfer the potatoes to a deep bowl and begin mashing with potato masher or fork. Whip the potatoes with a wire whisk, adding the butter, half-and-half, salt and pepper as you whip. Continue whipping until the potatoes are free of lumps. Serve hot, spooning the sauce for the goose over the potatoes.

For an attractive presentation, put the mashed potatoes into a large pastry bag with a large rosette tip and form mounds in a serving bowl. If the goose is to be served on a wooden platter, surround it with piped rosettes. Immediately before placing the hot goose slices on the platter, brown the rosettes under the broiler. Bring to the table immediately.

Broccoli on the Grill

SERVES 8

16   broccoli stalks, ends and leaves trimmed
2   tablespoons unsalted butter, at room temperature
$\frac{1}{2}$ teaspoon each salt and garlic powder

1. Wash the broccoli under cold running water. Arrange on sheet of aluminum foil large enough to completely cover broccoli to create a packet.

2. Dot broccoli with the butter. Sprinkle with salt and garlic powder.

3. Secure foil around broccoli, pinching all seams.

4. After removing goose from grill, place broccoli over drip pan. Cover and cook 10 minutes.

5. Remove from grill. Slit aluminum foil, being careful of escaping steam. Place in a serving bowl and serve hot.

Mock Mince Pie

SERVES 8

1   recipe crust (see Sweet Potato Casserole Pie, page 155)

MINCE FILLING

1   pound tart apples, peeled, cored and chopped
2   tablespoons all-purpose flour
½   cup sugar
¼   teaspoon ground cinnamon
¼   teaspoon ground allspice
¼   teaspoon freshly grated nutmeg
¼   teaspoon ground mace
1½ tablespoons grated lemon zest
3   tablespoons orange marmalade
2   tablespoons fresh lemon juice
2   tablespoons brandy
1½ cups golden raisins
¾   cup dried currants
2   egg yolks, lightly beaten
2   tablespoons unsalted butter for dotting top of pie

1. Preheat the oven to 350 degrees. Divide the crust dough in half. Place half in a 9-inch pie tin, rolling and patting the dough with your fingers until it extends past the edges of the pan. Prick the crust in several places and place a sheet of aluminum foil in the pie pan, pressing it down against the dough—this will help the dough to keep its shape in the oven.

2. Place the crust in the oven and bake at 350 degrees for 10 to 15 minutes or until cooked through but not browned. Remove from the oven and remove and discard the foil. Allow it to cool. Roll the remaining dough on floured wax paper into a 9-inch circle and place the wax paper on a cookie sheet. Refrigerate until needed.

3. Prepare the Mince Filling: Toss the apples with the flour in a large bowl. Stir in the sugar, cinnamon, allspice, nutmeg and mace. Then add the lemon zest, marmalade, lemon juice and brandy, mixing well. Stir in the raisins and currants, mixing well, then add the egg yolks and stir again to combine.

4. Preheat the oven to 450 degrees. Spoon the filling into the cooled crust and dot the top of the pie with the butter. Remove the 9-inch pie crust circle from the refrigerator and invert it onto the pie with the wax paper still attached. Carefully peel off the wax paper and press the edges of the pie lightly to fasten. Use a fork to decorate the edges if desired. Make 4 long slits in the top of the pie to act as steam vents.

5. Place the pie on the center rack in the oven and immediately lower the heat to 350 degrees. Bake for 45 minutes or until the top crust is nicely browned. Serve warm, cold or at room temperature.

Once More with Feeling

While we hope the recipes in this book are leftover-proof, even the best cooks are sometimes left with too much food. Here are some delicious recipes for yesterday's treats.

Don't feel bound by the type of poultry specified in a recipe. If a recipe calls for 2 cups leftover grilled chicken, the dish will be just as successful if made with a combination of any type of grilled poultry that equals 2 cups.

Chicken with Whole-Wheat Pasta and Pine Nuts

SERVES 6

This dish calls for wedges of fresh Parmesan and Romano cheese to be passed around the table with a cheese grater, allowing each guest to grate the cheese freshly onto his own pasta. Use only real fresh Parmesan and Romano, imported from Italy. Not only is the flavor superb, but only fresh Parmesan has that coarse-grained, crunchy texture.

1	tablespoon vegetable oil
1	teaspoon salt
12	ounces dried whole-wheat pasta
3	cups cubed leftover grilled chicken (or other poultry), skin and bones removed
¾	cup pine nuts
½	cup chopped scallions
4	tablespoons unsalted butter, melted
1	wedge fresh Parmesan cheese
1	wedge Romano cheese
	Freshly ground black pepper to taste
	Salt to taste
	Red pepper flakes to taste

1. Fill a soup kettle half full of water, add the oil and 1 teaspoon salt and bring to boil. Slide the pasta into the water and cook for about 5 minutes or until *al dente* (thoroughly cooked with no raw spots, but still offering some resistance to the teeth). Pour the pasta into a colander and immediately run cold water over it to stop it from cooking. Fill a pot half full of water again and bring to boil.

2. Preheat the oven to 350 degrees. Wrap the chicken in aluminum foil and place it in the oven for 10 minutes or until heated through. While chicken heats, toast the pine nuts: Place the nuts in a large, dry skillet in a single layer and set over medium heat. Cook for 1 minute, then stir often with a wooden spoon until lightly browned. Watch carefully so the nuts don't burn. Immediately remove them from the heat and allow to cool.

3. Pour the boiling water over the pasta to heat it and shake the colander to remove excess water. Quickly transfer the pasta to a serving platter with raised sides. Add the chicken, pine nuts and scallions. Pour in the melted butter and toss lightly to combine, coating the pasta.

4. Serve immediately, passing a platter with the fresh cheese wedges and grater. Pass pepper, salt and red pepper flakes.

Grilled Chicken Risotto

SERVES 6

3   tablespoons vegetable oil
2   cloves garlic, minced
1   large onion, thinly sliced
1   large red bell pepper, seeded and chopped
2½   cups leftover grilled chicken (or other poultry), cut into ½-inch cubes
4   tablespoons unsalted butter
1½   cups raw Arborio rice
3   cups chicken broth
¼   teaspoon salt
¼   teaspoon freshly ground black pepper
1   wedge fresh Parmesan cheese

1. Heat the oil in a large, heavy-bottomed frying pan. Add the garlic, onion and bell pepper and cook over medium heat for about 6 minutes or until softened, stirring occasionally. Add the chicken, combine well, then remove from the heat. Transfer the chicken and vegetables to a bowl and reserve.

2. Melt the butter in a frying pan. Add the rice and stir until the rice is coated with the butter. Add 1½ cups of the chicken broth, cover and simmer over medium heat for about 15 minutes or until the liquid is absorbed. Add the salt, pepper and remaining chicken broth. Cover and continue cooking until the rice is tender, about 10 minutes.

3. Stir the chicken and vegetables into the rice mixture and heat until

warm. Spoon the risotto onto a serving platter with raised sides and bring it to the table. Pass a platter holding the wedge of Parmesan cheese and a cheese grater so guests can grate their own cheese onto the risotto.

Warm Smoked Duck Salad with Garlic Croutons

SERVES 6

GARLIC CROUTONS

6 slices day-old white bread (use bakery bread if possible)

3 tablespoons unsalted butter

3 cloves garlic, minced

3 cups leftover smoked duck slivers, skin and bones discarded (or substitute smoked chicken or turkey)

6 slices bacon, cut into 2-inch pieces

18 ounces mixed greens: Romaine, Bibb, Boston or leaf lettuce, washed, dried and torn into bite-sized pices

2 large plum tomatoes at room temperature, cut into lengthwise slices

⅓ cup virgin olive oil

3 tablespoons red wine vinegar

¼ teaspoon salt

¼ teaspoon freshly ground black pepper

¼ teaspoon dried thyme

1. Prepare the Garlic Croutons: Remove the crusts from the bread and cut the slices into ¾-inch cubes. Heat the butter with the minced garlic. When sizzling, add the bread cubes. Sauté the bread cubes for about 5 minutes over medium heat, turning often with a spatula or wooden spoon. When the cubes are light brown, transfer them to paper towels.

2. Preheat the oven to 325 degrees. Wrap the duck slivers in foil and

heat them in the oven at 325 degrees for 10 to 12 minutes or until warm.

3. Fry the bacon slowly over medium heat for about 5 minutes or until crisp. Transfer the bacon to paper towels, drain and break into ½-inch pieces.

4. Arrange the lettuce pieces in the bottom of a salad bowl. Add the tomato slices and duck slivers. Toss the salad gently but thoroughly with the olive oil until all the leaves are coated. Mix vinegar, salt, pepper and thyme together in a small bowl and pour the mixture over the salad, tossing again in the same manner.

5. Sprinkle the bacon pieces and Garlic Croutons over the top of the salad. Serve immediately.

Smoked Turkey, Pecan and Fresh Raspberry Salad

SERVES 8

This salad is made with red leaf lettuce, red onions and red raspberries. Serve it in a glass bowl to show off its beautiful colors.

DRESSING

6   tablespoons raspberry vinegar
½   cup virgin olive oil
¼   cup Dijon mustard
¼   teaspoon salt
¼   teaspoon freshly ground black pepper

SALAD

2   large ripe pears, peeled, cored and julienned
2   tablespoons fresh lime juice
3   cups radicchio, washed, dried and torn into bite-sized pieces
1   red onion, sliced paper-thin and separated into rings
2½ to 3 cups julienned smoked turkey or chicken
¾   cup whole salted pecans
1   cup fresh raspberries, rinsed and dried carefully

1. Prepare the dressing: Combine the raspberry vinegar, olive oil, Dijon mustard, salt and pepper in a small bowl and reserve.

2. Toss the pears in the 2 tablespoons lime juice. Arrange the pears with the radicchio, onion rings, smoked turkey and pecans in an attractive glass serving bowl. Add the dressing and toss well to combine. Sprinkle with the fresh raspberries.

Chicken Tostadas with Hot Green Salsa

SERVES 6

This recipe calls for two unusual ingredients: cilantro (fresh coriander) and tomatillos, a vegetable that resembles red tomatoes but comes from a different family. Tomatillos are always cooked before eating. Both ingredients are sold at Mexican and other Hispanic food stores.

HOT GREEN SALSA

1   12-ounce can tomatillos, drained
1   small onion, quartered
3   jalapeño peppers, split lengthwise and seeded (see *Note*)
3   cloves garlic, peeled and halved
¼   teaspoon salt
¼   cup stemmed fresh cilantro

1   cup shredded lettuce
1   cup chopped tomatoes
1   cup shredded Monterey Jack cheese
2   cups leftover grilled chicken (or other poultry), shredded
½   cup chopped black olives
6   corn tortillas
     Vegetable oil for frying tortillas

1. Prepare the Hot Green Salsa: Place the tomatillos, onion quarters, jalapeño peppers, garlic, salt and cilantro in a food processor fitted with the steel blade and pulse several times until finely chopped. Transfer the salsa to a serving bowl.

2. Place the lettuce, tomatoes, cheese, chicken and black olives in separate bowls and bring the bowls to the table.

3. Pour the oil into the bottom of a heavy-bottomed, high-sided skillet to a depth of ½ to ¾ inch and insert a deep-frying thermometer. Heat the oil until it reaches 375 degrees. Slide a tortilla into the hot oil and cook until the tortilla is golden brown and crisp. This will take less than 1 minute. Turn the tortilla with tongs and cook until the other side is golden brown. Remove it from the oil and drain it on paper towels. Repeat this process with the remaining tortillas, cooking them 1 at a time.

4. Immediately arrange the fried tortillas on a serving platter and bring to the table. Guests should sprinkle each tortilla with layers of the ingredients in order: lettuce, chicken, tomatoes, cheese and olives. Top everything with the Hot Green Salsa.

Note: If possible, wear rubber gloves when working with jalapeños. If you can't, wash your hands afterward and be careful not to touch your eyes.

Grilled Chicken Muffuletta

SERVES 6

OLIVE SALAD

1¼   cups pimiento-stuffed olives plus ¼ cup liquid from the jar
¾   cup drained jarred roasted red bell peppers
2   small stalks celery, peeled, trimmed and cut into 1-inch pieces
       to measure ½ cup
3   cloves garlic
1   small onion, quartered
¼   cup virgin olive oil
⅛   teaspoon freshly ground black pepper

6   round kaiser-type rolls, preferably made of French bread
½   pound leftover grilled chicken or turkey, thinly sliced
6   ounces Genoa salami, thinly sliced
6   ounces Provolone cheese, thinly sliced

1. Prepare the Olive Salad: Place the olives, olive liquid, drained roasted peppers, celery pieces, garlic and onion in a food processor fitted with the steel blade. Pulse until the salad ingredients are finely chopped. Add the olive oil and black pepper, mixing well. Transfer the mixture to a bowl, cover and refrigerate until needed.

2. Preheat the oven to 325 degrees. Slice the round rolls horizontally and place the bottom slices on a foil-lined cookie sheet. Arrange a layer of chicken on top of the rolls. Then sprinkle the olive salad over the chicken. Place the salami slices over the olive salad. Top with the cheese slices. Put the top of the rolls in place.

3. Place the cookie sheet in the oven and heat at 325 degrees for 10 minutes or until the sandwiches are heated through and the cheese is melted. Serve immediately.

Chicken or Turkey Chili

This recipe can easily be doubled.

SERVES 4 TO 6

3   slices bacon

1   large onion, minced

3   cloves garlic, minced

3   tablespoons chili powder

1   teaspoon ground cumin

1   14½-ounce can crushed tomatoes with liquid

3   cups diced leftover grilled chicken or turkey

2   16-ounce cans red kidney beans, drained

1   10-ounce bag blue or yellow corn chips (optional)

1. Place the bacon in a 4-quart saucepan over medium heat and cook until brown—about 10 minutes. Remove the bacon and drain it on paper towels, patting with the towels to remove excess grease.

2. Add the onion and garlic to the bacon fat and cook for about 5 minutes, stirring occasionally. Crumble the bacon and add it to the saucepan with the chili powder, cumin and tomatoes. Simmer for 5 more minutes.

3. Stir in the chicken or turkey and beans and cook for another 5 minutes. Serve immediately with corn chips on the side for sprinkling over the individual chili bowls if desired.

Appendix

Mail-Order Sources of Ingredients

As of December 1988 you could write to or call the following companies for catalogs or price lists.

Anzen Pacific Imports
7750 North East 17th Street
P.O. Box 11401
Portland, OR 97211
(503) 283-1284
Japanese, Chinese, plus some
   Korean, Thai and Vietnamese
   ingredients

Carolyn Collins Caviar
P.O. Box 662
Crystal Lake, IL 60014
(815) 459-6210
American caviar and roe

Conte di Savoia
555 West Roosevelt Road
Jeffro Plaza–Store #7
Chicago, IL 60607
(312) 666-3471
Mostly Italian and European,
   but some Middle Eastern and
   Japanese ingredients

Food Stuffs
338 Park Avenue
Glencoe, IL 60022
(312) 835-5105
European and American gourmet
   and specialty ingredients

The Forsts
12-2410 Broeck Avenue
Kingston, NY 12498
(914) 331-3500
Tame game and other birds

Griffo-Grill
301 Oak Street
Quincy, IL 62301
(217) 222-0700

Holy Land Grocery, Inc.
4806 North Kedzie Avenue
Chicago, IL 60659
(312) 588-3306
Middle Eastern ingredients

House of Spices
76-17 Broadway
Jackson Heights, NY 11373
(718) 476-1577
Indian ingredients and all
   spices

Iron Gate Products, Inc.
424 West 54th Street
New York, NY 10019
(212) 757-2670
Game and other birds

The Oriental Food Market
2801 West Howard Street
Chicago, IL 60645
(312) 274-2826
Chinese ingredients

Pete Casados of Casados Farms
P.O. Box 1269
San Juan Pueblo, NM 87103
(505) 852-2433
Blue cornmeal, blue tortilla
chips and chili caribe

Star Market
3349 North Clark Street
Chicago, IL 60659
(312) 472-0599
Japanese ingredients

Uwajimaya, Inc.
519 6th Avenue South
Seattle, WA 98104
(206) 624-6248
Japanese, Korean, Chinese plus
some Vietnamese and Thai
ingredients

Wild Game, Inc.
2315 West Huron Street
Chicago, IL 60612
(312) 278-1661
Farm-raised wild game, including free-range chicken and
turkey and poussin

Index